the top 100 CANADIAN singles

Also by Bob Mersereau
The Top 100 Canadian Albums

the top 100 CANADIAN singles

Bob Mersereau

GOOSE LANE

Printed in Canada on FSC certified paper.
10 9 8 7 6 5 4 3 2 1

Library and Archives Canada Cataloguing in Publication

Mersereau, Bob, 1960-
        The top 100 Canadian singles / Bob Mersereau.

Includes index.
ISBN 978-0-86492-537-4

        1. Popular music — Canada — Discography. 2. Popular music — Canada — History and criticism. I. Title. II. Title: Top one hundred Canadian singles.

ML3484.M575 2010   781.64'0971   C2010-904913-6

Written by Bob Mersereau
Produced by Susanne Alexander & Goose Lane Editions
Susanne Alexander: vocals, tambourine
Julie Scriver: art direction, pianos/synthesizers, vocals
Kent Fackenthall: cover & book design, drums
Ann Marie Brown: logistics, banjo, pedal steel
Viola Spencer: booking & financial management, guitar, fan club management
Corey Redekop: tour management & publicity, percussion, background vocals
Angela Williams: artist relations & legal management, bass, background vocals
Nick McCaig: shipping & receiving, harmonica, cowbell, triangle
Edited & mixed by Barry Norris
Proofread & engineered by Lisa Alward
Vinyl management Jaye Haworth and Julie Scriver
Singer artwork on the cover by Michael Newell, who appears courtesy of iStockphoto
Goose Lane Editions would like to thank all the artists, labels, & management that provided artwork (and music) for this project. Rock on.
Goose Lane Editions acknowledges the financial support of the Canada Council for the Arts, the Government of Canada through the Book Publishing Industry Development Program (BPIDP), and the New Brunswick Department of Wellness, Culture and Sport for its publishing activities.

Recorded & mixed during the summer of 2010 at
        Goose Lane Editions
        Suite 330, 500 Beaverbrook Court
        Fredericton, New Brunswick
        CANADA E3B 5X4
        www.gooselane.com

Now I've heard there was a secret chord
That David played, and it pleased the Lord
— Leonard Cohen, "Hallelujah"

There's nothin' better for your soul
Than lyin' in the sun and listenin' to rock 'n' roll
— Lighthouse, "Sunny Days"

Bon c'est bon, bon, bon, c'est bon, bon
— The Stampeders, "Sweet City Woman"

Introduction

Bob Mersereau
Fredericton, 2010

Welcome to *The Top 100 Canadian Singles*, a companion book to 2007's *The Top 100 Canadian Albums*. To all who enjoyed that first work, I hope you find just as much interesting material here and perhaps are introduced to some new favourites. I encourage everyone to listen again, or for the first time, to all these wonderful songs. If you put them all in order, as I have, on your MP3 or iPod, you'll have one of the best playlists ever, no matter what country you're considering.

The aim of this book is much the same as that of the *Albums* project: to celebrate Canadian music — in this case, the great singles we've heard over the years, from 78 rpm shellac discs to today's Internet downloads. Once again, Goose Lane Editions presents the book in an attractive coffee-table format, with a vibrant design, original artwork, and vintage photos. We've treated this music as it deserves, as some of the best art this country has produced.

Another goal is to stir up debate, conversation, and recognition of these and other fine Canadian songs. It's a list book, compiled by a large jury, but none of you will completely agree with the final one hundred chosen. Art is arbitrary — we knew that going into the project. But everyone involved hopes you will have fun with the list, and any debate and argument that occurs will just prove the point that there are many, many great Canadian singles.

I knew there would be debate about *The Top 100 Canadian Albums*, but I certainly wasn't prepared for the amount, or for the intensity of opinion with which the book was greeted in October 2007. It certainly touched a nerve with the press and readers alike. Almost every media outlet in the country devoted significant space to the announcement of the Top 100 albums. There were full-page features in national and major daily newspapers, dozens of radio talk shows devoted to it, and polls and contests on websites. I found myself making a string of appearances on TV and radio shows from British Columbia to Newfoundland and Labrador, along with a non-stop series of phone interviews for papers, websites, and magazines. There were launches in big bookstores and readings in tiny local libraries. The TV show *This Hour Has*

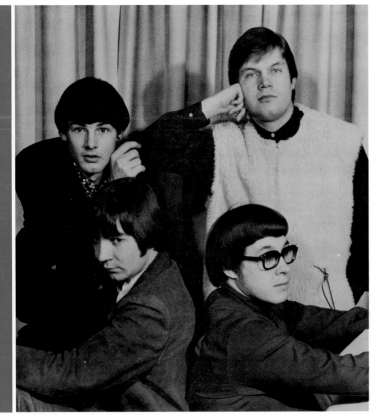

The Guess Who: Burton Cummings, Jim Kale, Garry Peterson, and Randy Bachman.

22 Minutes based a joke around the book. George Stroumboulopoulos tried to bribe Prime Minister Stephen Harper into coming on his show with a free, autographed copy of the book (it didn't work). I joined Daniel Lanois for part of a tour, as a sort of opening act, peppering him with questions for the audience about his album *Acadie*, which finished at #20.

Of course, not all the reaction was positive. Many people were upset that their favourite artists weren't included. Like so many other arguments in this country, it was often a regional concern. Nova Scotians were annoyed that there were no Anne Murray or Hank

Snow albums in the Top 100. In British Columbia, there were calls for everyone from Payola$ to Spirit Of The West to The New Pornographers. In Quebec, it was shock and outrage that the list omitted Pagliaro, Charlebois, and Beau Dommage. All I can say is, check out the list of the Top 100 singles.

In the end, our theory was right. Canadians did want a list of some of their favourite albums, they did want to see them treated as fine art, and they did want to have lots of discussions and debate. The book became a national bestseller, was updated a year later for a soft-cover edition with new interviews and material, and has remained a constant seller.

The big news for this book is that Canada has a King of the Single. Although Neil Young dominated the *Albums* book, with eight selections in the Top 100, in this book, Randy Bachman is the clear winner. You'll find his hands all over *The Top 100 Canadian Singles*, at #1 with The Guess Who and "American Woman", as well as a further three more singles with that band, two more with Bachman-Turner Overdrive, and another two as producer of Trooper. Bachman has mastered all the main jobs: over the past forty years he has been a musician, lyricist, lead singer, lead guitar player, producer, and frontman for major touring bands. He works in pop, hard rock, and jazz. And he has a second career as a successful broadcaster on CBC Radio.

For *The Top 100 Canadian Singles*, we used the same basic format and ideas as for the *Albums* book. Once again, the list was chosen by a survey of music fans across the country. You'll recognize many of the names of the jury. Many are directly involved in the daily creation, sales, promotion, and broadcasting of Canadian music. There are famous musicians, well-known media people, managers, record company employees, reviewers, writers, deejays, retailers, roadies, and club owners. And there are also lots of just plain fans who love Canadian music and make it a part of their daily life. I think we've got a good cross-section of Canadians from every region, whose cumulative choices reflect a pretty accurate picture of the most-loved Canadian singles ever made.

Once again, we've included the choices of some celebrities, one of whom also delighted us in the *Albums* book: Bubbles, of the hit TV show the *Trailer Park Boys*, who was too important an expert on Canadian music to leave out, so once more he brings his own unique spin on the best songs.

For the articles on each song, rather than relying on old quotes that could be taken out of context or were inaccurate in the first place, I again chose to present clear and fresh perspectives on the works through all-new interviews with the artists or with people directly associated with them. They have some fascinating stories to tell.

When deciding how to present this book, I had to make three major decisions. The first involved the very heart of the book. During the first promotional tour for the *Albums* book, I was asked constantly, during interviews and question-and-answer sessions, what the next book would be. There were lots of suggestions, from the top hundred songs to the top hundred bands, the top hundred songwriters, even the top hundred Canadian heavy metal songs. I quickly decided the follow-up book should be about individual songs. But should it focus on songs *per se* or on those specifically released as singles? In the end, I decided on singles, partly because polls of the best songs had been done a few times before, most notably in 2005 on CBC Radio's *50 Tracks*, hosted by Jian Ghomeshi, when listeners

chose Ian & Sylvia's "Four Strong Winds" as the best Canadian song of all time.

I liked the idea of singles. It followed albums nicely, and for many people there's magic in their youthful memories of hearing those great hits on the radio. I grew up thrilled by the Top Forty, of discovering bands such as Lighthouse, April Wine, and The Stampeders via the airwaves. Plus, I simply love the format: that small piece of vinyl with the big hole in the middle, spinning at 45 rpm. They cost ninety-nine cents in those days and came with a song on each side and sometimes a picture sleeve cover. I still collect 45s, own a jukebox, and like nothing better in the world than scouring through a shoebox at a yard sale for that rare gem.

And that led to the second major decision. In the digital age, does the single still exist? True, in physical format the single is almost dead, the 45 rpm disc having been replaced by cassettes, CDs, and finally downloads

Eric's Trip, launch of *The Top 100 Canadian Albums* book, Halifax, 2007.

Neil Young, Bob Mersereau, and Elliot Roberts (Young's manager), Halifax, 2008.

of computer files. But to me, the answer is a resounding yes. In fact, everything is a single now, as any song can be purchased individually. Singles are still released by the hundreds each week, as new albums come out and artists and record labels urge broadcasters and website operators to play certain tracks. Many consumers have stopped searching out albums by their favourite artists and now concentrate on buying just the tracks they have heard and liked. In many ways, the single is more important than ever. And it still costs ninety-nine cents.

In presenting their selections for this book, jurors were instructed to pick songs that had been released as singles, whether to the public for sale or to broadcasters in some sort of medium for airplay. It could be an audio release, such as a CD single, or a video issued to TV stations. This eliminated some favourite Canadian songs from contention, but it didn't seem to matter much in the end: the vast majority of our most-loved songs have been released as singles at some point. The book also includes a few double-sided hits, where both sides of the 45 single did well on the charts — a fairly rare accomplishment and one worthy of recognition.

The final decision I had to make went to the heart of Canada's national identity: the existence of two official languages and two almost separate music worlds. The reality is that anglophone Canadians rarely know or listen to the artists and music of French Canada, while francophones listen to lots of English-Canadian music: they know Bryan Adams as well as they do Jean Leloup. So comparing the two music worlds is like comparing *pommes* to oranges.

The Top 100 Canadian Albums received much criticism for its lack of francophone content: just four French-language albums and the bilingual *Acadie* by Daniel Lanois. On a proportional basis alone, francophone Quebec artists should have accounted for at least a fifth of the albums list. But the list reflected the choices of those polled. Quebecers tended to vote for both francophone and anglophone artists, or they assumed that, since the book was to appear in English only, they should choose only English-speaking artists. Moreover, those Quebecers who did choose albums by francophone artists split their votes in many ways. In English Canada, in contrast, having been bombarded over the years by critics and publications from Canada, the United States, and Britain assuring them that *Blue* and *Harvest* are among the best albums ever made, most people included these Joni Mitchell and Neil Young albums in their choices.

Ultimately, it was an almost impossible task to present a list that would please all Canadians. At first, I thought I ought to make separate lists of the Top 100 English and Top 100 French singles. But that would have made for a book that was too large, or for articles that were much shorter. I felt, though, that if I wrote only about anglophone artists, I would lose an opportunity to present to my mainly English-speaking readers some culturally important francophone artists. So, in the end, I settled on that most Canadian of solutions: a compromise. *The Top 100 Canadian Singles* includes a few by francophone artists — indeed,

Joni Mitchell, Vancouver, 1970.

anglophone jurors seemed somewhat readier to vote for certain classic francophone singles than they were to include albums. Plus, you'll find a separate, unannotated list of the "Top 100 French-Canadian Singles," to underscore the fact that musical talent knows no boundaries in this great country of ours.

In soliciting votes for *The Top 100 Canadian Singles*, I invited all those who submitted their choices for *The Top 100 Canadian Albums* once again to take part. Most did so, and they were augmented by many new voters. Those polled were asked to vote for their Top 10 singles, but almost everyone had the same response: only 10? This turned out to be a tough job — much tougher than choosing ten albums. Some gave up, some cursed me, others stretched the deadline to the last minute, some changed their minds days or even weeks after first submitting their choices. To everyone

who took part, for all your hard work and enthusiasm, I offer my thanks.

Lastly, my greatest pleasure was interviewing so many of the fantastic artists this country has produced. Some I had met several times before, others I was enjoying talking to for the first time. All were free and open with their memories, most of them very happy ones. There were so many good stories and quotes that each of the singles deserves a book of its own, rather than the small space allotted to it here.

I hope you enjoy the stories and fun memories of the artists who created *The Top 100 Canadian Singles*. If one of your own favourites is not on this list, go ahead and fight among yourselves. Call me names; I can take it. After all, you'd only be proving that some of the best music of all time has come out of Canada, and there's no shortage of it.

1 American Woman/ No Sugar Tonight

The Guess Who
RCA, 1970

Accidents will happen. No matter how much planning and rehearsing musicians do for their stage show, something's bound to go wrong at some point. Fireworks and light shows and giant screens make rock concerts exciting, but there's always going to be one time on a tour when a major glitch threatens to derail the whole concert, or at least wreck the mood. Maybe the lead singer's microphone goes dead. Perhaps the local guy hired to run the spotlight leaves his intercom switch open by mistake, letting the booming music flood all the tech crew's headsets, causing confusion and panic as no one can hear their cues. Okay, I'm the guilty party on that one, messing up during a Loverboy–Bryan Adams gig in 1981. It didn't end up hurting their careers any, but it did end my roadie days pretty quickly, steering me toward broadcasting. You see, it's not the mistakes that matter, it's how you react to them.

The biggest mistake in Canadian pop music led directly to the greatest success. It was 1970, and The Guess Who were the top band in Canada. But in those days, even top bands could be stymied by the smallest of accidents, like the one that happened to guitar player

Randy Bachman. "As the legend goes, and it's true, The Guess Who were playing a gig in a curling rink in Kitchener-Waterloo," he confirms. "I broke a string, and Burton Cummings announced that the band would be taking a break while I changed my string. I had no guitar tech, spare guitar, or even a tuner, so I put on the low E string, went over to Burton's electric piano, kneeled down in the dark, and started tuning my guitar to his piano. I started to play the riff, and heads in the audience jerked around. I stood up and kept playing the riff. The band, sensing something going on from my head motions, came on stage and we started to jam that riff. Burton came up and played a flute solo, a harmonica solo, and then starting singing the opening line."

"American Woman" wasn't as yet a song, or even a work-in-progress. Bachman is emphatic that he had never played the signature opening guitar line before that night: "No, no, no, I had not written the riff before." The band had recently returned from a US tour, and Cummings was tired of the negativity in that country because of the Vietnam War, racism, and the "generation gap." That's why he wanted

American women (and men) to stay away. Bachman knew the group had just created a monster hit by accident, and remembers the feeling forty years later: "Yes, I will never forget that moment of electricity, decided to put them back-to-back like The Beatles had done with 'A Day In The Life'. Besides putting them back-to-back, we were able to superimpose the first verse of 'No Sugar Tonight' over the first verse of

"The opening of this song is what starts the motor of Canada's greatest rock song."

— Dale Robertson, Universal Music

when something hits you and you are a conductor that passes on the current of creation to the audience. The feedback when you are all on that plane is quite amazing." The buzz spread from the curling rink to the radio waves. "American Woman" topped the charts in Canada and the United States. That's a good place to end a story, with a song at number one, but in this case there was more success on the flip side.

Just a few months earlier, The Guess Who had enjoyed the rare achievement of a two-sided hit single, when "Laughing"/"Undun" scored on the radio. Now they were looking at another. As listeners to his CBC Radio show "Vinyl Tap" know, Bachman is a student of the music charts and pretty competitive when it comes to the numbers. "The Beatles and Creedence Clearwater Revival had many of these and we were thrilled when RCA listed 'American Woman'/'No Sugar Tonight' as a double A-side. They were both listed at number one on the Billboard charts in May 1970."

Making "No Sugar Tonight" a hit was a bit tricky. It was actually two songs, "No Sugar Tonight" and "New Mother Nature," melded together — the oddest Bachman and Cummings collaboration ever. "I had 'No Sugar Tonight' and he had 'New Mother Nature'," says Bachman. "They were both short songs and, not for lack of trying, we couldn't find a suitable bridge for either song. Both songs were in the same key, so we

'New Mother Nature' when we repeated them at the end of the song. It was a magical moment. It's great when you have an off-the-wall idea and try it against all common sense, and it works."

It might have worked for the *American Woman* album, but that was too complicated for Top Forty radio. Producer Jack Richardson edited "No Sugar Tonight" out of the medley. "He felt it was a more commercial track for radio," says Bachman. "Remember, in those days, bands had long cool tracks on FM album radio and much more commercial songs as singles on Top Forty radio. The trick was to have them both."

Randy Bachman and The Guess Who had them both — had it all. Bachman had also had enough of The Guess Who, and quit as the hits were riding at the top. But by this time, he'd learned how to survive all the accidents in the music world, and in four short years he'd repeat all of this success.

2 Heart Of Gold

Neil Young
Reprise, 1972

"Neil was there from the start, and
unlike his songs, I'm getting old."

— Dan Reynish, CBC Radio

Milestone or millstone? Neil Young has struggled with the huge success of his most beloved song ever since it topped the charts in 1972, propelling him to worldwide fame and fortune. It's a song he has disavowed publicly more than once in his career, yet he's fallen back on the fame of the "Heart Of Gold" sound whenever he wanted to placate his audience. "Heart Of Gold" represents the folkie, hippie Neil so beloved of his more casual fans, those not willing to follow him down his louder, darker paths or his many experimental phases. Just when it seems he might be losing his lustre, Young grabs an acoustic and blows those famous harmonica lines, and all is forgiven.

Back in 1972, Young was already famous and starting to enjoy the perks of rock royalty, thanks to his association with Crosby, Stills & Nash and a pretty decent hit the year before with his own *After The Gold Rush* album. Yet it was nothing compared to the fanfare the *Harvest* album received. Released in the heyday of the singer-songwriter craze, Young found himself at the top of a very successful genre along with his good friends James Taylor, Joni Mitchell, and other mellow

voices such as those of Cat Stevens and Carole King. Big money was starting to pour into rock as well, with record sales now counted in configurations of platinum instead of gold. An outsider like Young suddenly found himself part of the machine, a cash cow for big companies and promoters. While he had always been connected to his audience, especially through live shows, Young certainly wasn't a team player when it came to business.

His reaction to the number one status of "Heart Of Gold" was the start of a long line of wilfully destructive career moves. He sums it up best, and famously, in the liner notes to 1977's retrospective *Decade* collection: "This song put me in the middle of the road. Travelling there soon became a bore so I headed for the ditch." Hit the ditch he did, following up his biggest album with some of his poorest-selling and most fan-frustrating works. *Journey Through The Past* was the soundtrack to a bizarre film he made that few saw, featuring mostly old material and outtakes in raw form. *Time Fades Away*, a live album of all-new material from the tour that followed the success of "Heart Of Gold,"

out for the midnight singalong. Yet, like most Neil Young songs, the words are plain but the meaning is obscure and out of focus. It's no simple love song; instead, Young portrays himself as a desperate romantic, trying to find his one true heart of gold. He was only twenty-six when he recorded the song, yet he's already worrying he's getting old as he searches. He was more of an old soul, really.

Audiences first heard the song live in a medley with another well-loved but sometimes confusing *Harvest* number, "A Man Needs A Maid". As heard on the *Live At Massey Hall 1971* CD release, Young performed the new songs on piano, but soon separated them into their better-known versions. The original connection, though, helps to explain their lyrics. Young is searching for his love, his life's companion, and no, he's not looking for somebody to cook and clean for him — he's baring his heart of gold for all to see here. He's afraid, he needs that partner, and doesn't want to do it alone. Tellingly, the original live version of "Maid" features the lyric, later expunged, "afraid, a man feels afraid." Like most of Neil Young's work, there's a lot more going on beneath the surface.

In later years, Young seems to have come to terms with "Heart Of Gold". By 1992, he was willing to play on the success of *Harvest*, returning to the sound and many of the original 1972 players for the hit album *Harvest Moon*, which became his biggest-selling release since the 1970s. He brought out the acoustic again in 2005 for *Prairie Wind* — like *Harvest* and *Harvest Moon* a Nashville production, completing a trilogy of sorts. A live concert performance of the album at Nashville's Ryman Auditorium was released as a film called *Heart of Gold*.

By 2007, Young had put together a new group that came to be known as His Electric Band. This quintet,

was a collection of jarring rockers and bleak piano ballads. In one year, Young had driven away most of the new fans he'd won with *Harvest*.

"Heart Of Gold" seems simple enough on the surface. It's easy to sing, easy to remember, even easy and basic for novice guitar players. It might be the ultimate campfire classic — that one song every strummer, from teenagers to aging boomers, can pull made up of old hands that include original "Heart Of Gold" player Ben Keith, long-serving bassist Rick Rojas, and Young's wife, Peggy, is perhaps his most versatile group yet. They can handle the fireworks with "Rocking In The Free World" and "Cinnamon Girl", dig deep into the catalogue for surprises such as a "Tonight's The Night" mini-set, and join in on the acoustic tunes. Night after night, though, the biggest applause comes after the shock of recognition for the beloved standard, "Heart Of Gold", which he almost always includes — it's no longer a will-he-or-won't-he proposition. People don't complain anymore when he introduces brand-new works into the set — it's expected. The applause for a Grunge rocker like "Hey Hey, My My" is the same as for the banjo-driven "Old Man". And "Heart Of Gold"? For Neil Young, it's an old, best friend, a heavy burden finally lifted. Now he can be any kind of performer he wants to be on stage, quiet or loud, experimental or classic, and he's appreciated.

MY TOP 10 CANADIAN SINGLES

John Roberts

John Roberts anchors *American Morning* on CNN. Based in New York, Roberts began anchoring CNN's flagship morning program in April 2007. Previously, Roberts served as CNN's senior national correspondent. He spent fourteen years with CBS news, during which he served as chief White House correspondent and chief medical correspondent, anchor of the weekend editions of the *CBS Evening News*, and anchor of the *CBS Morning News*. Of course, in Canada, he'll always be known as J.D. Roberts, one of the veejay stars during the glory days of CITY-TV and MuchMusic. Always proud of his Canadian heritage and music journalism past, Roberts was more than pleased to weigh in with his favourite songs.

1. **AMERICAN WOMAN – The Guess Who**
   The first HUGE Canadian hit — the ultimate "living in the shadow of the elephant" song.

2. **SPIRIT OF RADIO – Rush**
   This song really embodied the shift away from "corp-rock radio" to a new attitude — less formulaic, more grassroots.

3. **LIFE IS A HIGHWAY – Tom Cochrane**
   Tom is such a great songwriter, guitarist, and a good friend. I love his original of this song with the harmonica, though I'm sure Tom appreciates the "Rascal Flatts retirement fund" version.

4. **SUZANNE – Leonard Cohen**
   A terrific offering from Canada's music poet laureate.

5. **LOVERS IN A DANGEROUS TIME – Bruce Cockburn**
   I interviewed Bruce many times about his passion for Central America. It struck me that this song grew at least partially out of his frustration with the wars and violence there.

6. **YOU OUGHTA KNOW – Alanis Morissette**
   Any time you want to be reminded why you should remain true blue to your relationship, give this one a spin . . . frightening.

7. **CRIMINAL MIND – Gowan**
   Larry is such a tremendous artist and songwriter.

8. **ROCKY MOUNTAIN WAY – Triumph**
   A great version of the Joe Walsh classic. Rik Emmet's opening guitar riff sounded spectacular bouncing off the back wall at Maple Leaf Gardens.

9. **ONE WEEK – Barenaked Ladies**
   Just plain good fun at a party trying to sing along.

10. **THE WRECK OF THE EDMUND FITZGERALD – Gordon Lightfoot**
    This was on the charts while I was a disc jockey at CHUM Radio. An unlikely Top Forty hit, but a plaintive, soulful tribute to those lost in the deep icewater locker of Superior.

3 The Weight

The Band
Capitol, 1968

"This is the greatest story ever told. Sorry, God."

— Evan Newman, manager

In 1967 Levon and The Hawks were adrift. After a controversial and stressful tour with Bob Dylan, the group's members headed to his hideaway home near Woodstock, New York, on retainer and on hiatus, as Dylan convalesced after his motorcycle accident. Drummer Levon Helm wasn't even around, having quit the Dylan gig because of all the booing the electric music was receiving from the folk fans. With nothing else to do, keyboard players Garth Hudson and Richard Manuel, plus bass player Rick Danko, rented a big pink house near Woodstock, and guitar player Robbie Robertson found digs nearby. The pink house was big enough to accommodate long days of playing and recording, and soon Dylan started coming by, working on new material with the group.

This music was far different from Dylan's sounds of 1966 — a much looser and lighthearted series of songs that became known and partially released as *The Basement Tapes*. Dylan was enjoying the spontaneity and the down-home roots music they were creating, and worked up novelty numbers such as "The Mighty Quinn". Meanwhile, the rest of the group, four

transplanted Canadians, were inspired to write on their own, and sometimes with Dylan, developing a new group identity.

With Dylan still reluctant to tour, thoughts turned to an album project for the as-yet-unnamed group. Helm was talked back into the family, and brimming with confidence and a parcel of tunes, the quintet, now calling themselves The Band, started work on what became *Music From Big Pink*.

That's when music producer John Simon came into the picture. He was developing a strong reputation as the producer for Simon & Garfunkel, Leonard Cohen, and Gordon Lightfoot. Another of Dylan's, and his manager Albert Grossman's, projects slowly evolving in Woodstock was filmmaking, and Simon had been brought in for that, but he soon was transferred to oversee The Band's work. "Howard Alk, who was a moviemaker, and more, from Chicago, had been on the Dylan tour before Bob's accident," explains Simon. "He and I were editing *You Are What You Eat*, a movie by Peter Yarrow and Barry Feinstein, in a house in Woodstock. One night I heard a godawful sound.

It was Garth, Rick, Richard, and Robbie serenading Howard on his birthday on instruments they could barely play. Howard knew the guys wanted to record, but the tape he was familiar with was a sort of a goof from *The Basement Tapes* period called 'Even If It's A Pig, Part One', and all he knew of my work was an album based on Marshall McLuhan's *The Medium Is The Message*. Both projects were sort of Dada so he figured we were a good match. It was serendipity: we were a good match, but for musical and songwriting reasons."

Producer and engineer Simon served as a sixth member of the group, forming the all-important horn section with Garth Hudson. He was immediately impressed with the group, and shares his first impressions: "Wonderful. Different. Deep. Musical. Respectful of tradition."

Simon also got a surprise with the new songs the group intended for their debut album. Instead of the casual and comedic work he'd first been exposed to, he was presented with a set of fully formed, wonderful originals, including an unrecorded Dylan original, "I Shall Be Released", a Dylan–Richard Manuel number, "Tears Of Rage", and Dylan and Danko's "This Wheel's On Fire". It was a treasure trove. "I don't think I liked one of them over the others," offers Simon. "They were all great."

The album, however, would not be made at Big Pink. Instead, Simon transferred the group to New York City: "In the old Columbia Records Studio A, 799 Seventh Avenue, a room I was very familiar with. Of course [the musicians were] all in one room, on four-track tape, mostly all live. The only things we overdubbed were, for instance, on 'Tears Of Rage', the horns and the tambourine." These are some of the most important group arrangements in modern popular music, the template for roots-rock bands ever since, and they were achieved quickly and perfectly, live to tape.

Despite the heavyweight presence of Dylan's songs on the album, it was one of the group's own, "The Weight," that caused the biggest sensation and was the only single from the album. Writer Robbie Robertson has described the lyrics of the song as a type of North American mythology with which he was experimenting, influenced by his interest in avant-garde filmmakers. There are biblical allusions throughout, including the place name of Nazareth, a Miss Moses, a stranger seeking a bed, Luke, and Judgment Day. Plus, musically, it's a gospel number, featuring spiritual-like triplet

vocals in the chorus, directly inspired by the music of gospel group The Staple Singers. All that, yet still it's just a little story with no big message. It's simply an incredible use of language, imagery, and melody, a song that resonates out of time. It is a song no one tires of, a delight to hear each and every time.

It was almost thrown away. Robertson has said the group didn't even rehearse it going into the studio. They weren't sure if it was something that could make the final cut, which John Simon confirms. "I think 'The Weight' could've been 100 per cent live," he remembers. "It was the last song we did, different from the others. Sort of an afterthought, maybe." So casual

was the process, Simon still didn't know he had helmed one of the most important records, and singles, of all time. He didn't even know he had an album at that point. "The songs were a demo for Albert Grossman to get a deal for them. I just liked the music and the experience a lot — more than any of the many projects that I'd done before."

While it was not a hit single in its time, "The Weight" is now considered by music fans and musicians as one of the most important artistic creations that a (mostly) Canadian group has produced.

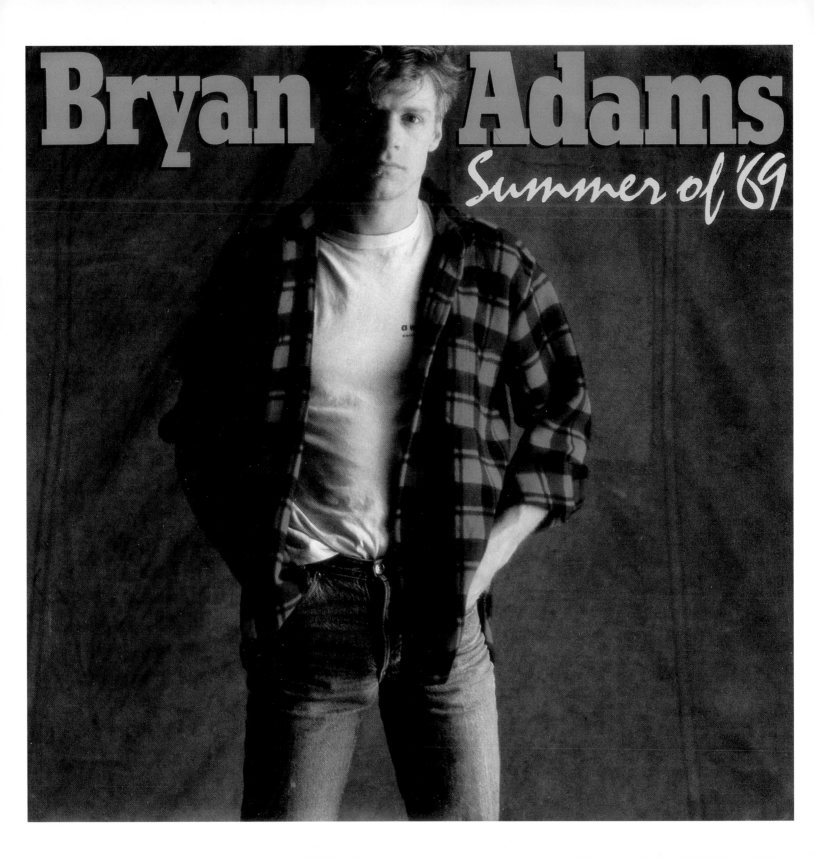

4 Summer Of '69

Bryan Adams
A&M, 1985

"The first chord is enough to bring Canadians to their feet."

— John Wiles, CKBW

As chronicled in *The Top 100 Canadian Albums*, a chance introduction at Vancouver's Long & McQuade music store in 1978 led to the most successful songwriting partnership in Canadian rock history. Jim Vallance and Bryan Adams would work almost every day for the next eleven years, learning and eventually perfecting their craft. Vallance, seven years Adams's senior, was impressed with his confidence. Vallance had recently left the rising group Prism, while Adams had fronted Sweeney Todd. Within a few days of meeting, they'd written the disco hit "Let Me Take You Dancing". Better songs lay ahead.

The Adams-Vallance partnership lasted until 1991 and the *Waking Up The Neighbours* album. But by 2005, the writing relationship was rebuilding. In 2008, Adams's album *11* was released, featuring three new Adams-Vallance compositions. This time, the two weren't sitting knee-to-knee in the basement. Instead,

it was a long-distance session, with Adams in different countries and Vallance in Canada, the pair sending MP3 audio files back and forth by email.

That system worked well for songwriting so Bryan, Jim, and I used it for *The Top 100 Canadian Singles*. For the four Adams singles featured in the Top 100 list, we chatted via email in an exclusive interview with the men behind the songs. While "Summer of '69" might not have been the biggest chart or sales hit of their career, both men agreed with our voters about its enduring popularity.

Bob Mersereau: Should this be considered your top hit?

Bryan Adams: Without a doubt. I love it, too. Someone in Spain recently asked me why I wrote the lyric, "I got my first real sex dream". I corrected him.

Jim Vallance: Whenever I've seen Bryan in concert — Canada, England, wherever — this is the song that gets the biggest reaction from the audience.

BM: Where did you come up with the story in the song?

BA: The song was originally called "Best Days Of My

Life", and it was kind of a mixture of ideas about growing up and nostalgia. The main thing about the story was I wanted to be able to sing about something real, like I did buy an electric guitar at a five-and-dime in Ottawa, and the characters in the song, Jimmy and Jody, are people I worked with at the time. Jody still works for me. I also liked the ambiguity of the number 69 and the connotations and the possible double entendre it had; the yin and yang and the blatantly obvious sexual reference.

JV: "Best Days Of My Life". . . that was the name of the song. It took a few weeks to realize that "Summer Of '69" was a better title. So we literally shoehorned that phrase into a few gaps in the arrangement. In 1966, John Lennon and Paul McCartney challenged each other to write a song about their childhood in Liverpool. Paul came up with "Penny Lane" and John wrote "Strawberry Fields Forever". Bryan and I decided we'd try something similar and write about growing up in Canada in the sixties. We both had guitars at an early age and we remembered playing "'til our fingers bled." We were both in bands with classmates, and we had crushes on girls in high school. Once we started discussing those memories, we had the beginnings of a storyline.

BM: What's the magic of this song? Is it the story being told?

BA: First of all, it's got a great up-tempo rock groove. It's a coming-of-age song so the lyrics are identifiable to most. Jim had said to me at some point that he'd seen the film Summer of '42, and I remember adding "back in the summer of '69" as an ad lib after the line "those were the best days of my life." I suppose it just didn't sound finished to end on what we thought was the title. Hence a new title was born, and a better one.

JV: I was seventeen in 1969. It was an amazing year. I watched the moon landing on TV. Woodstock happened. There were new albums from The Beatles, The Band, Led Zeppelin. With "Summer Of '69", we tried to convey what it was like for us, growing up in the sixties.

BM: It's a classic opening line, "I got my first real 6-string." Did you always have that, or was there a moment when somebody said, hey, this could start with . . .

BA: It's just what happened, the story needed to start from the beginning.

JV: I've always loved authors like Joseph Conrad and Katherine Mansfield. I like how their stories just "start," as if the action is already under way.

BM: Other writers have told me that nostalgia is often a key ingredient in a hit song. "Those were the best days of my life . . ." Thoughts on that?

BA: Nostalgia sneaks its way into many of our songs. It's great to be able to write about things that happened, but most of our songs were so simple and so concise that anyone could think that it was part of their lives. I think that was one of the secret ingredients to our songs. They were very "everyman."

BM: Bryan's had hits with rockers and ballads; which did you guys prefer to write?

BA: We liked both, and wrote both hit ballads and hit rockers.

JV: For songwriters, changing tempo keeps it interesting — a ballad one day, a rocker the next.

MY TOP 10 CANADIAN SINGLES

Paul Quarrington

It was a thrill to find out that writer and musician Paul Quarrington would be reviewing my first book, *The Top 100 Canadian Albums*, for the *Globe and Mail*. To have him say it was "well written" meant more to me than any other praise or comment. Among his many accolades, Quarrington was the winner of the Governor General's Award for Fiction in 1989 for his novel *Whale Music*. He was a recognized educator, journalist, playwright, screenwriter, and musician. The first time we met, Paul was playing with his group The Porkbelly Futures on an East Coast tour. A good talk ensued, followed by some emails and then an invitation to submit a list to this book. On Canada Day, 2009, The Porkbelly Futures were once again playing in Fredericton, so I got a chance to talk to Paul some more and, to my great pleasure, was able to inform him that a song he co-wrote, Rheostatics' "Claire", had been voted as the #42 song in *The Top 100 Canadian Singles*. Sadly, Paul passed away from cancer January 21, 2010, before he was able to pass on his comments about the songs he chose for his Top Ten. But here is the list he compiled.

1. OPPORTUNITY – The Mandala

2. WHEN I DIE – Motherlode

3. CLAIRE – The Rheostatics

4. SOMETIMES WHEN WE TOUCH – Dan Hill

5. SEASONS IN THE SUN – Terry Jacks

6. BRAINWASHED – David Clayton-Thomas and The Bossmen

7. NOTHIN' – The Ugly Ducklings

8. IF I CALL YOU BY SOME NAME – The Paupers

9. INSENSITIVE – Jann Arden

10. BABY AND THE BLUES – Quarrington/Worthy

5 Hallelujah

Leonard Cohen
Columbia, 1984

On May 11, 2008, Leonard Cohen began one of the most surprising and delightful comebacks in the history of popular music. He took the stage of The Playhouse in Fredericton, New Brunswick, on the first night of a world tour — his first tour in fifteen years. He was seventy-three years old, and many people had naturally assumed he would never hit the road again. The tour continued on to the great stages and festivals, including London's O2 Arena, the Glastonbury Festival, and the Coachella Festival. The tour continued for two years, with Cohen turning seventy-five.

Audiences have numbered in the thousands and tens of thousands — that is, unless you were in Fredericton or the other Maritime dates on the warm-up portion of the tour. That opening night, Cohen played to just under seven hundred people, including your writer in the seventh row. Cohen, a little nervous, walked on stage to the first of several standing ovations. With his usual modesty, he thanked us warmly and proceeded to thrill his old and new fans with a greatest hits

performance. I remember feeling it must be one of the two or three best concerts I'd ever seen. I also thought I might be caught up in the emotion of the event, but the sentiment has been echoed now many times by writers and fans.

While there were many highlights, the biggest thrill was when Cohen began "Hallelujah". This was something new, for the audience and for the performer.

> "This is simply the best song ever written, anytime, anywhere!"
>
> — Jaymz Bee, JAZZ.FM

In the past, this honour has been reserved for "Suzanne", "Bird On A Wire", or perhaps later songs such as "I'm Your Man" or "Tower Of Song". This time, there was a rush of excitement when "Hallelujah" began, and another standing ovation. By a strange route, twenty-six years after he first recorded it for an ignored album, *Various Positions*, the song has become Cohen's most popular number.

Ironically, for a book about singles, "Hallelujah" wasn't one at first. Its status now as one of the top Canadian singles shows how the very definition of a single has changed, and speaks to the new power of the Internet, film soundtracks, downloads, and

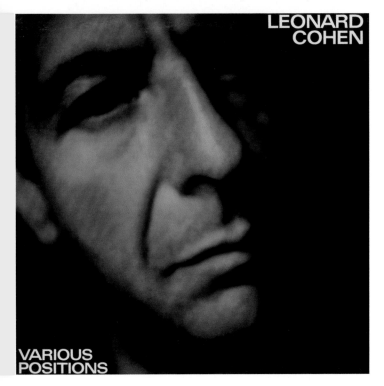

cover versions. It appeared as the B-side of a single in Europe when *Various Positions* was released, but there wasn't much interest in a new Cohen single in 1984. The album was greeted with indifference at best and outright refusal in the United States, where Columbia initially declined to release it. Cohen's career was at its lowest mark. Even in Canada, where he was still regarded with respect, few bothered buying the record.

In 1987, Cohen's fortunes began to rise again. His long-time backup singer and sometime collaborator Jennifer Warnes recorded a tribute album, *Famous Blue Raincoat*, which was a strong success. A new generation of fans became familiar with his work, and overnight, you could feel Cohen becoming hip again. By the following year's *I'm Your Man* album, he was the toast of thinking people's rock, cutting a suave figure on video channels with his suits and shades and sexiness.

Around that time, a few musicians were catching up with *Various Positions*, which by then had become more readily available in the United States. "Hallelujah" was starting to find an audience. Bob Dylan played it live, and it was a highlight of a 1991 tribute album to Cohen, *I'm Your Fan*, as interpreted by famed Velvet Underground founder John Cale. That opened the floodgates, with performers around the world covering the song at an ever-increasing rate. It helped push newcomer Jeff Buckley to quick stardom in 1994 with his album *Grace*. Cale's cover showed up in the movie *Shrek*, although on the soundtrack disc a Rufus Wainwright version was used. k.d. lang included it on her *Hymns Of The 49th Parallel*. Cohen told me, during my interview with him for *The Top 100 Canadian Albums*, that lang's live performance of the song was his favourite cover. lang was touched by the compliment, but passed it on: "I think the definitive version is Jeff Buckley's. Everyone and his dog has sung 'Hallelujah' to this point, but I really think it's because of Jeff Buckley's version, defining that song to the public."

Cohen feels, however, that the song has become over-recorded, and has even suggested a moratorium might be in order. Here's why. In the annual competition to have the number one single in England at Christmas, three different versions of "Hallelujah"

placed in the charts there in December 2008, with reality show contestant Alexandra Burke's at number one, Buckley's at number two, and Cohen's own, based solely on download sales, at number thirty-six.

I asked Cohen's long-time friend Warnes to weigh in on the popularity of the song and her favourite version of it. "As a child, I was taught the word Alleluia, (spelled without an h or a j) from the original Greek, I believe. This word is sacred among students of Gregorian chant because it functions as a doorway or a portal to something greater than ourselves. So few words have the power to alleviate (alleluia) our feelings of separation from God, or help us imagine what eternity must be like. This is one of those words. The

Greek section of Montreal is not far from the Cohen family home, and Leonard also keeps a home on the island of Hydra. Leonard knows the real meaning of this word in any form. Maybe Leonard wanted such a word to be returned back into the hands of ordinary people, living ordinary lives. . . . John Cale's version of Leonard's 'Hallelujah' satisfies me more than other versions, because John grew up understanding the original Greek meaning, and to my ear he sings and plays this song like an insider."

So take your pick, whether it's Jeff Buckley's, k.d. lang's, John Cale's, or Cohen's own, there's no doubt "Hallelujah" has become one of the world's most popular songs.

6 Born To Be Wild

Steppenwolf
Dunhill, 1968

One of the most popular acts in the mid-sixties Yorkville Village scene in Toronto went by a somewhat confusing series of names. The Sparrows backed singer Jack London on a series of singles before striking out on their own with a new leader, John Kay. Around this time, the name was shortened to The Sparrow, or just Sparrow. Kay, a German-born émigré, had moved to Canada and then to the United States with his parents, but as a budding performer had been attracted back to the Yorkville scene. The group enjoyed moderate success touring the United States, but by 1967, in Los Angeles, it had fizzled out.

There, Kay recalled several of the Sparrow members and formed a new band that became Steppenwolf, still mostly made of Canadians. Here the names continue to get confusing. Sparrow drummer Jerry Edmonton (whose real name was McCrohan) was called in. His brother Dennis followed, but instead of going by McCrohan, or Edmonton as he had in Sparrow, Dennis now called himself Mars Bonfire. Plus, he had decided he wasn't interested in being in Steppenwolf. He had other plans.

Mars Bonfire still lives comfortably in California. "Being in The Sparrow gave me a chance to observe and participate in many aspects of the music business," he explains, "such as being a musician, producing music recordings, creating songs, arranging music, running a recording studio, and more. What ended up appealing to me the most was songwriting, so much so that I decided to concentrate entirely on that and let go of being a musician."

For musicians and songwriters, LA was one of the best places to be in 1967. The record labels had been convinced that rock music was a fad. But, by then, they realized that rock singles and albums were outselling anything else they could produce, and the groups were becoming the new, young stars. For budding songwriter Mars Bonfire, that meant freedom, excitement, and something else that went with living in LA: a new car.

"A Ford Falcon," he remembers — the first car he ever owned. "The Sparrow had a vehicle for getting ourselves and our gear to clubs, but I had no transportation of my own and saw nothing of California except motel rooms, night clubs, and

Hollywood. When I got the Falcon I drove to the ocean, to the mountains, and to the high desert, and I was amazed and thrilled with the beauty and diversity of southern California." Hence the opening line of the song: "Get your motor running, head out on the highway, looking for adventure in whatever comes our way."

It was the humble Ford Falcon, not a souped-up T-Bird or a Harley-Davidson that directly inspired the ultimate rock highway song. Of course, it didn't matter what ride Bonfire owned. "I was simply trying to capture some feelings I was experiencing as a result of my new freedom to drive and discover. My brother Jerry called me several weeks after the song was written and asked me to bring over some songs for his new band, Steppenwolf. I put together a tape of several songs, including 'Born To Be Wild', and went to visit him a few days later."

Then came a close call, one so serious it could have changed the entire future of rock music. The dog almost ate his homework: "Jerry wasn't home so I dropped the unboxed tape through the mail slot in his front door. Then I immediately heard the sound of his Great Dane running towards the door, barking and agitated. I walked away certain the dog had mangled the demo tape and that was the end of it. To my surprise, I learned the tape survived the dog, the group liked some of the songs, and they chose 'Born To Be Wild' as the first one to work on."

Good dog. The Dane had just saved a Top Ten hit, an anthem of the 1960s, an iconic tune still used today by any movie or TV show looking to telegraph the mood of escape. Oh, it might even have been the place Heavy Metal music got its name, from the lyrics. Bonfire explains where he got that term: "I first heard the term heavy metal as a category of the periodic table when I was studying science. During my Falcon ramblings I experienced some thunderstorms in the mountains. The darkening of the sky, the flash of lightning, and the crack of thunder prompted the phrase, 'I like smoke and lightning, heavy metal thunder.' I have been told that a music reviewer for *Rolling Stone* was the first to use the phrase to describe music similar in intensity to that of Steppenwolf."

As big a hit as the song was on first release, its status as a classic came the next year when it became the key song in the hit film *Easy Rider*. Bonfire says it was a perfect place for the song. "I was thrilled. It gave a captivating imagery to the words of the song that is similar to what was going on in my head when I wrote it. I ride a KTM off-road motorcycle and 'Born To Be Wild' runs through my head every time I jump on the kick-starter. The song and the movie work together to enhance their mutual success. Every young person, at some point, has feelings as simple and elemental as those I had that inspired the song and many can make a connection to the mood and imagery of 'Born To Be Wild', even though music styles have changed."

So remember kids, it doesn't matter how cool your first car or motorbike is; it's all about the freedom. Because he captured those moments behind the wheel of a Ford Falcon so powerfully, Mars Bonfire's song has been a hit for every generation since.

"An American rock anthem for the ages, immortalized in a classic American film — surprise!"

— Bob Reid, CFRB

Denise Donlan

The executive director of CBC Radio, Donlan has had a pivotal career in broadcasting and music in Canada. As a music journalist, she brought serious and thoughtful stories to air on CITY-TV and MuchMusic's *The New Music*. She also became the director of music programming and then vice-president and general manager of Much and CITY. Thanks to her dedication to Canadian music, she's considered instrumental in the success of many of the acts who came to fame via Much. In 2000, she became president of Sony Music Canada, and has been a terrific advocate, organizer, and fundraiser for several charities. She's also married to a Canadian music treasure, one of the artists on her list below. See if you can guess whom.

BRUCE COCKBURN

MURRAY MCLAUCHLAN

1. **CHILD'S SONG – Murray McLauchlan**
   Because it always makes me cry and I know the story so well!! :-)

2. **CANADIAN RAILROAD TRILOGY – Gordon Lightfoot**
   Because it's so IMPORTANT and I believe was actually a song commissioned by the CBC.

3. **RIVER – Joni Mitchell**
   Reminds me so strongly of Canada and Joni's genius.

4. **SOUTHERN MAN – Neil Young**
   Such a strong, necessary cry for justice, and because he got Lynyrd Skynyrd to answer back!

5. **TRY – Blue Rodeo**
   I always remember the power of this song breaking on MuchMusic, and Jim still hits it out of the park!

THE TRAGICALLY HIP

6. **BOBCAYGEON – The Tragically Hip**
   So many Hip songs to choose from, but this one paints a vivid picture, and who else would write about Bobcaygeon?

7. **RISE UP – Parachute Club**
   A significant human rights anthem with past, present, and future power.

8. **CLOSER TO THE HEART – Rush**
   I've been a Rush fan forever, and while it's hard to pick a Rush favourite, at least in this one, my air drums aren't so lame!

I loved the Tsunami relief version with Ed Robertson and Bubbles.

9. **FALL FOR ANYTHING – Jeremy Fisher**
   I signed Jeremy on the strength of this song and believe him when he says, "If you don't stand for something, you'll believe in anything"!

10. **ROSE OF JERICHO – Liam Titcomb**
    This song truly shows the strength of Liam's songwriting. A Rose of Jericho is apparently a dust bowl plant that revives and flowers instantly with water, and Liam seems to have that effect on so many things!

    and just because it should always go to "ELEVEN" . . .

11. **LITTLE LAMBS – Marc Jordan**
    Because it always makes me cry.

7 If You Could Read My Mind

Gordon Lightfoot
Reprise, 1970

> "I thought he was a great talent, he just needed exposure and seasoning."
>
> — Ian Tyson

Here's the difference between Canadian music fans and US or British music fans. We understand Gordon Lightfoot. We consider him one of the top songwriters of his generation, on par with Neil and Joni and Leonard — maybe even Dylan himself. But cross the border or the ocean, and the critics scoff. He's remembered for a couple of seventies hits and lumped into the singer-songwriter scene of that decade.

So let's have Dylan speak about his friend. Asked about his current favourite songwriters in 2009, Dylan offered the names of John Prine, Warren Zevon, Randy Newman — and Lightfoot. He mentions "If You Could Read My Mind" and "Sundown", and says, "I can't think of any I don't like." On another occasion, Dylan said when he hears a Gordon Lightfoot song, he wishes it would never end.

I mention these compliments to Lightfoot, who is resting at home in Toronto after another lengthy tour, and tell him Dylan called him "Gordo." "That's what they called me around the office," he laughs. "You see, we had the same manager. He's been very kind to me all these years. He also called me the Pavarotti of the folksingers."

But you, Canadian music fan, don't need Bob Dylan to tell you of Gordon Lightfoot's greatness. His songs are part of our cultural identity, and perhaps best represent our unique connections with nature, solitude, history, and humility that come from living in such a huge northern land. Gordon Lightfoot's voice is like the call of the loon — it reaches directly into my Canadian soul.

In 1970, Gordon Lightfoot was a well-known songwriter, but he'd never been a force on the pop charts. That was about to change, but it took a moment of profound sadness to inspire "If You Could Read My Mind". "I remember writing it really well, the afternoon I wrote it," says Lightfoot. "It was a one-day thing. I had many songs like that. I could see that my marriage was going downhill, which it did about a year later. All of a sudden the words came to me. I found out I was writing about an upcoming event, a life-changing event that was going to take place for me personally, and it did. So it's the story really, about the demise of a marriage if you want to be direct about it. It was spontaneous, it only took a couple or three hours to write. The words were falling into place.

I was writing them down, and they were just falling right out onto the paper."

Although open to discussing it now, Lightfoot was less direct in discussing his marriage in the song. Instead, he set the song in a movie script, complete with castles dark. "That's all movie stuff. I'd seen the Magic Castle in Hollywood. I remember getting a vision of that place while I was writing the song. It was a magic place, where all the artists were magicians. It was sitting up on the south side of the Hollywood Hills, and it looked like a little castle sitting up there. I found out it was a club. I went up there one night to have a look, and I saw some pretty good magic tricks up there, too.

"I was just thinking about a replacement for an ailing relationship, I brought the movie angle into it. I don't know where this stuff comes from. It's impossible to invent some of this stuff, it has to fall out of you. And you have to be in some kind of an emotional state.

I found emotional trauma, which I've had most of my life because I've been through two or three marriages now, had a lot to do with it, because it used to find its way in when I shouldn't have been able to write at all, just through remorse and through grief. Yet there it was. It was the escape, you know?"

At first, it wasn't considered as a single, let alone a potential hit song. Lightfoot had just started an important new record deal, and had delivered a major song about the Vietnam War called "Sit Down Young Stranger". His new album was named after that song at first, until "If You Could Read My Mind" took off. "It was a sleeper song," Lightfoot says. "It laid on an album for eight months before it got picked up by the promotion department at Reprise. I certainly wasn't going to complain about it — that was my very first album with Reprise, and they were treating me as a folk artist. They didn't expect it, they hoped there might be a single there, but they certainly weren't pressuring me to do anything in that regard."

As the single climbed the charts, the months-old album was reissued, now titled after the hit song. Lightfoot didn't see any of this coming. "I was very much surprised, yes indeed I was. I didn't think it was a particularly good recording of it. I'd have loved to have another shot at it — I do it three times as good now. I don't actually like the recording of it, I don't like my performance, basically. But there's something about the lyric of that song I think that was very strong, and I think it was really the lyric that got the message over with that one. I was able to get away with having a weak arrangement and not a very good vocal."

That's pretty harsh criticism for one of the top Canadian singles of all time, but Lightfoot's hearing something you and I aren't in his voice. "I probably stayed up half the night, you know, the night before

I recorded it. I had just gotten into LA when I did that session, and I think that I'd met up with a couple of old buddies and was drinking 'til about three o'clock in the morning before I recorded that one."

8 Takin' Care Of Business

Bachman-Turner Overdrive
Mercury, 1974

> "Ask anyone who loves to labor at nothing all day and they'll tell you that this peerless power pop paean to self-employed sloth has it all."
>
> – Jeffery Morgan, *CREEM*

Randy Bachman should be called the Professor of the Pop Single. Since the early sixties, he's studied what it takes to make them and each little trick. He mastered instrumental guitar rock, British Invasion, Top Forty, psychedelic, FM hits, and country rock in the bands Chad Allan and The Expressions, The Guess Who, and Brave Belt. The Guess Who could mimic anybody on the charts, as they proved on their weekly CBC-TV show *Let's Go*, playing magpie versions of everyone from The Doors to Cream to The Beatles.

Sometimes what Professor Bachman was crafting came out a little too close to the originals he had studied. Take the case study of a song he started back in The Guess Who days: "I wanted to write a 'worker' song. The song I wrote to model 'Johnny B. Goode' and 'Paperback Writer' was called 'White Collar Worker'. The verses were the same, but in the middle the song stopped, and I sang 'White Collar Worker'. Imagine that being sung like the break in 'Paperback Writer'. So of course, nobody liked this song. This was back in '67 or '68. I pitched it to Burton and The Guess Who, but it was too close to 'Paperback'."

Years pass, Bachman leaves The Guess Who in 1970,

has little luck with his next group, Brave Belt, and eventually forms the harder-rocking Bachman-Turner Overdrive. Having hit the top with The Guess Who, Bachman wanted back in, another shot at chart success. He knew it took a lot of hard work to get there, and BTO played everywhere and anywhere in North America. Bachman was back in the bus, like a former major league all-star attempting a comeback in the minor leagues. He needed another big hit.

"Fast-forward to the early seventies, I've moved my new band to Vancouver, and Bachman-Turner Overdrive are playing clubs in the city. I pitch 'White Collar Worker' to record companies and no one wants to touch it. One night driving to the club gig, the deejay on the radio said, 'Hi. This is Darryl B. and we're taking care of business on CKLG.' I knew Darryl from Winnipeg and thought, great title for a song. That night at the club when (Fred) Turner lost his voice and I had to sing a bunch of songs in the last set, I pulled out the verses to 'White Collar Worker' and thought I'd drop the hook in the middle and see how 'Takin' Care of Business' would fit in. This was done on-stage with no discussion with the band. I was desperate to keep the people dancing. I just started the song, sang the old verses, and magically 'Takin' Care of Business' fit right in the space. It was done on-stage, live, like 'American Woman'. A few weeks later, we recorded it." Again, similar to the creation of our number one single, "American Woman", a happy, unplanned accident, leading directly to one of the world's most popular hits.

To heck with this professor business — with two positions in the Top 10 of our Top 100 Canadian Singles, Bachman should be known as the King of Canadian Hits. And the other King was quick to pick up on Randy's tune, too: "I saw Priscilla Presley on an HBO special and they asked her that question. She said she and the gang were with Elvis in the car in Los Angeles, going to the airport. 'Takin' Care Of Business' came on the radio by a Canadian band, and Elvis said, 'Wow . . . I love that song . . . I love that title . . . I wanna use that for my slogan'."

Bachman's list of songwriting credits reads like the playlist on your local classic rock radio station. For BTO, "You Ain't Seen Nothin' Yet" was actually a bigger worldwide hit, plus there's "Let It Ride", "Hey You", "Roll On Down The Highway", and more. "Dunrobin's Gone", the lone Brave Belt near-hit, received a considerable amount of votes in the poll for this book. Then there are all The Guess Who hits he wrote or co-wrote. Yet he can quite easily pick his favourite of all these: "Has to be 'Takin' Care Of Business'. The whole world rocks to that song everywhere I go."

There's no greater celebration of Canadian pop music than the Bachman-Cummings road show, which features all The Guess Who hits, BTO songs, and Burton Cummings solo numbers. For Bachman, it's the ideal showcase for all their combined material: "Touring with Burton Cummings is just plain fun. We know each other so well, and together and separately,

we kind of wrote the book on pop and rock music from the Canadian point of view and sent it out to the world to rock."

So, does Randy Bachman have the golden touch, does he hold the secret to writing and recording hits? "There's a secret and there's no secret. It's one of those intangible things. Most of my hits have been accidents or incidents that I've learned to stand back and watch as a spectator in a way. I'm amazed at how some of them come to be. So, part of the secret is to 'let a song happen.' Knowing when to relax, stop forcing it and let it flow from wherever it's coming from to you. Get it, capture it, remember it, and use it. Then there is the formula of listening to the radio and trying to write like the songs you like that are getting played at the moment, and they usually reflect public taste of the moment. Although radio and trends are a moving target, it's a good exercise to try to write a follow-up to a hit on the radio."

There you have it, folks, as close to the secret of pop success as you're going to get.

Rich Terfry

A.k.a. Buck 65, Terfry leads a double life as one of Canada's outstanding musicians and the host of CBC Radio 2's *Drive* show, heard Monday to Friday afternoons. He's a huge fan of pretty much everything.

"Putting this list together was utterly agonizing for me. Limiting it to only ten meant leaving off some of the most important songs in my life. In the end, I based my Top 10 on the songs I've listened to the most, even if I could argue that others were better in one way or another. So it's more personal favourites than what I think is best. It's also impossible to rank them, so I'll list them alphabetically by artist."

ARCADE FIRE

1. **NEIGHBOURHOOD #3 (POWER OUT) – Arcade Fire**
   This song has a sense of urgency about it that few can match. First time I heard it, I lost my mind.

2. **BACKTEETH – Elevator Through Hell**
   Plain and simple, this is one of the heaviest, most menacing things I've ever heard. And I've always had a thing for heavy menace.

3. **SUNDOWN – Gordon Lightfoot**
   I feel macho when I listen to this song, which is saying something for a wimp like me.

4. **SUGARCANE – Hardship Post**
   If someone challenged me to put a song up against "Smells Like Teen Spirit" by Nirvana, this is what I'd choose.

5. **LET THERE BE DRUMS – The Incredible Bongo Band**
   I've never been 100 per cent sure of how Canadian this band was, but the record has the MAPL label on it. It was my favourite song when I was a little kid, when it was the theme music for Atlantic Grand Prix Wrestling.

6. **LIFE IS UNBELIEVABLE – John Southworth**
   Nothing I know of inspires in the face of a world gone wrong like this song. JS is a genius.

7. **SUZANNE – Leonard Cohen**
   My whole list could have been Leonard Cohen songs. Nobody touches him lyrically.

8. **LOOKING AT THE FRONT DOOR – Main Source**
   One of the best hip-hop songs ever recorded. Masterpiece.

9. **OLD MAN – Neil Young**
   I've been haunted by this song since the first time I heard it when I was a baby.

SLOAN

10. **COAX ME – Sloan**
    It's kinda too bad the Consolidated reference will always pin this song to the early nineties. But otherwise, it's one of my favourite songs ever.

Honourable mentions:
AHEAD BY A CENTURY – The Tragically Hip; ROMANTIC RIGHTS – Death From Above 1979; ANY SENSE OF TIME – The Inbreds; I'VE BEEN EVERYWHERE – Hank Snow; MUSHABOOM – Feist; WALKING WITH A GHOST – Tegan and Sara; THE JOY OF COOKING – Old Man Luedecke; DREAMER – Jenn Grant; HERE IS WHAT IS – Daniel Lanois.

9 Four Strong Winds

Ian & Sylvia
Vanguard, 1963

> "Both of us, me and Ian Tyson, we were both inspired directly by Dylan. If he can do it, so can I — that's what Tyson said when he wrote 'Four Strong Winds'. I was thinking that way when I wrote 'Early Morning Rain'."
>
> — Gordon Lightfoot

When Ian & Sylvia started out in the folk scene, the performers didn't write the songs. The folk boom of the late fifties and early sixties featured artists covering material from decades past, songs which had been passed down for generations, searched out and restored to popularity by scholars and collectors. Some might be centuries old, brought from the British Isles. Others came through African American sources, passed on from player to player — blues, jazz, or gospel. That's what the new Canadian duo were doing in Toronto, with the added bonus of the occasional Quebec folk song.

First, they watched as the club scene changed in Yorkville. "The folk song was starting to make inroads into the jazz scene that was there," remembers Ian Tyson. "And the jazz guys weren't too happy about that. The clubs started to appear just like mushrooms overnight, the Village Corner, the Purple (whatever it was), Onion, or something. It's fading in my memory now. It became huge in a couple of years."

Ian & Sylvia became bigger. The top stars of the local scene, they were ready to make the move to where the real action was, to the heart of the folk boom, New York's Greenwich Village. "It was the Big Apple," says Tyson. "It was just beginning, it was a fledging scene that we were at the beginning of, in the Village. It was pretty open. Everybody was green. People came from everywhere, Oklahoma, and the Midwest, the South, up in Maine, and the ones that made it made it. Record companies were signing up these folkies. Vanguard made an offer, and we took it. By and large, [the albums] were pretty good. The first albums sold very well."

The duo's debut album, *Ian & Sylvia*, followed the folk purist's format of traditional material. With so many acts getting in on the folk boom, there were only a limited number of these songs to perform, and the musicians borrowed each other's songs and arrangements, always on the lookout for something fresh. In 1962, everything changed. Ian Tyson, like several others in the Village, became friendly with a new talent, Bob Dylan. Although Dylan knew lots of the same folk and blues songs, and his first album was almost all covers, he did have the audacity to start writing his own songs, like his hero and friend Woody Guthrie. Soon the Village was abuzz with word of major new songs Dylan was performing.

Ian & Sylvia knew the game had changed. Their manager, Albert Grossman, also handled Dylan and Peter, Paul and Mary. He'd had the trio record Dylan's "Blowin' In The Wind", and it sold a million copies. Everybody was getting rich off these new folk songs. Ian Tyson knew he couldn't be a singer and interpreter any more: "I'd written songs before, but they weren't recorded. The first one that I said, well, I can write a song? Well, I'd have to say 'Four Strong Winds'."

Dylan had a song about the wind, so Tyson borrowed the image. That's where the comparisons end. Using the tried-and-true advice of write what you know, Tyson came up with a character he knew well from Canada, a migrant worker. He would have run into them in his various jobs in British Columbia, Alberta, and Ontario, working the rodeo or the clubs. He explained the song's genesis in the liner notes to the *Four Strong Winds* album: "Canada has many seasonal workers, and when the weather turns harsh they must move on and find a different type of work. Many of these people cross the country every year — from the tobacco harvest in Ontario to the wheat harvest on the prairies to apple picking in British Columbia. With the advent of fall they move on, perhaps to return with the spring."

Bravely, Tyson kept the song in Canada, famously naming Alberta in the lyrics, a place most Americans couldn't point out on a map. In an industry where Canadians are still advised to take out the local references if you want to break through in the United States, Tyson's journeyman tale has set the standard for true patriot songwriters ever since, from Rheostatics to The Tragically Hip to Joel Plaskett.

The song did become a big hit but not for Ian & Sylvia, at least in the United States. It took a cover version by country singer Bobby Bare in 1964 for it to enter the Top Ten — in the country charts. In Canada, however, Ian & Sylvia's version became a national hit. It then took on a life of its own, first becoming a standard for the duo's fellow folk performers and then simply becoming a classic song. Among the dozens of cover versions, it's been recorded by Johnny Cash, Joan Baez, Judy Collins, Hank Snow (note the lyrical similarity to Snow's "I'm Movin' On"), John Denver, Sarah McLachlan, and, with the biggest compliment, Dylan himself, bringing it all back home.

The best-known recording around the world is by Neil Young, since it was one of two songs he chose to perform at The Band's farewell concert, The Last Waltz, in 1976. Feeling especially patriotic in the company of Ronnie Hawkins, Joni Mitchell, and members of The Band, he chose, instead of one of his many gems, a Canadian classic. Released as a single in 1978, Young's version was only a minor pop hit, but became a major fan favourite and introduced a whole new generation to "Four Strong Winds". Young's appreciation of the song has never waned. He continues to play it in concert to this day, the only cover version that has stayed a permanent part of his repertoire.

Perhaps the ultimate tribute has come from Canadians themselves. In 2005, CBC Radio took a poll on the program *50 Tracks*, asking listeners to vote for the greatest Canadian song of all time. They chose "Four Strong Winds".

Aaron Pritchett

One of the biggest country stars in Canada, Vancouver native Pritchett's hits include "New Frontier", "Big Wheel", "Hellbent for Buffalo", and 2006's "Hold My Beer", the Canadian Country Music Association's Song Of The Year. Although country is his main gig, Pritchett grew up surrounded by all types of music, loves Elvis and Stevie Wonder, and listens to everything from hip-hop to symphonies to jazz. He says his Top 10 list is in no particular order.

1. **HOME – Michael Bublé**
   I loved this song from the first time I heard it. I thought it was only because he was from my hometown of Vancouver, but it's because this song is brilliant, in my mind, and he's an amazing vocalist.

2. **JUST BETWEEN YOU AND ME – April Wine**
   I remember hearing this song when I was a kid around the time I had my first girlfriend. It was my first love song.

3. **MY OWN WAY TO ROCK – Burton Cummings**
   My parents listened to this record of Burton's a lot, but I really dug it and used to play it in the band.

4. **BIG LEAGUE – Tom Cochrane & Red Rider**
   Being a hockey player all my life and knowing a young boy who passed away while playing hockey back in the eighties, I really related to this and always thought it was a great song.

5. **WE'RE HERE FOR A GOOD TIME (NOT A LONG TIME) – Trooper**
   The ultimate party tune for Canadians . . . or for anyone in this world!

ALANIS MORISSETTE

6. **YOU OUGHTA KNOW – Alanis Morissette**
   Alanis mentioned that she channelled the songs on *Jagged Little Pill* and they were all great, but for radio, I think this was the best one.

7. **NEW ORLEANS IS SINKING – The Tragically Hip**
   I didn't know what to think of The Hip when I first heard them, but then I got it and thought they were the coolest new sound I had heard in 1990.

8. **TRY – Blue Rodeo**
   This was the first BR song I'd ever heard and I thought, if this is what all their music is like, then I'm a fan . . . and still am today because of "Try".

9. **HOW YOU REMIND ME – Nickelback**
   I love that this song started the whole Nickelback phenomenon and when played, it still gets people riled up!

10. **THESE EYES – The Guess Who**
    Again, a Burton Cummings song that I grew up listening to on vinyl on a record player that was the size of a '72 Gran Torino. This is a song that I still have on my music player today that is the size of a breath strip. Although the ways of playing music have changed drastically, one thing has remained the same: there will always be great Canadian music!

10 Snowbird

Anne Murray
Capitol, 1970

"Gene MacLellan's best, but without Anne's touch, likely would have gone unnoticed."

— J.C. Douglas, Newcap Broadcasting

Maritimer Anne Murray had decided to give up her teaching career at the end of the 1960s and try to make it as a singer. She'd already had lots of national exposure, thanks to her TV appearances on the popular *Singalong Jubilee* and her 1968 debut album, *What About Me*. At that time, she first heard about Prince Edward Island songwriter Gene MacLellan and his song "Snowbird". "There's some confusion as to where I first heard it," says Murray. "I wrote in my autobiography that I first heard it at the CBC in Halifax, but a friend has since told me he remembers me seeing Gene perform it in his lounge in Charlottetown."

Murray had no doubts about the song, and wanted to record it right away. "I liked it immediately," she confirms. "At that time, I didn't have the experience to pick out a good song, but I knew. I think it was just a visceral reaction to the song. I knew that I really liked it. I lived with it and 'Bidin' My Time', which was the other song he gave me. I lived with those over the summer, and I loved them both. Gene was a true poet. The pictures that he could paint with very few words were just great."

The song made Anne Murray an international star. A Top Ten hit in both Canada and the United States, it launched her onto American TV, where she became a regular guest on singer Glen Campbell's program and his duet partner for several hits and albums. In addition, she became a regular guest on network talk shows and the star of several Canadian TV specials. It also created her image, which she has kept to this day — that of a sweet, small-town Canadian girl, flying into the States from the frozen north. "It did define me," she says now. "And I had never even heard of a snowbird, I didn't even know what it was. It's a snow bunting that he was writing about." Remarkably, the term snowbird entered the Canadian vernacular to describe the many well-off Canadians who can afford to live part of the cold winter in Florida. The song also had a life apart from Anne Murray's. It immediately became a pop standard, covered dozens of times, most memorably by Elvis Presley, who considered Murray's version his favourite record at the time. That's an achievement Murray still cherishes to this day.

It also made a star, of sorts, of its writer. Murray's

success with "Snowbird" and "Bidin' My Time" soon made Gene MacLellan a recording artist in his own right. His "The Call" became a radio favourite, and the group Ocean had a huge international hit with his gospel number, "Put Your Hand In The Hand", much to Murray's chagrin, as she had wanted it for herself. But MacLellan was never comfortable with fame. His daughter, Catherine, is now one of the country's finest young performers, in the proud tradition of Maritime singer-songwriters. Growing up, she knew "Songbird" had been a mixed blessing for her father. "My dad and I had never talked too much about the song," she says, "and how he felt. I know sometimes he felt a bit of a mix between the burden of having to play it every time he performed and gratitude at being able to have attained that level of success. I know he was definitely pleased with the success Anne Murray had with the song. It gave him the ability to sit back and write without having to perform and be in the spotlight as much. My dad really shied away from the spotlight, he was such an introspective, quiet guy, and in the end all the attention wasn't good for him." MacLellan died in 1995.

But the attention was good for other aspiring musicians in the Maritimes, including his daughter. "My dad never let himself be too proud of anything he did," says Catherine. "He was such a humble man, he wouldn't take any of that to heart if he could help it. I do know, though, that all of the Maritimers were proud of him. And a lot of up-and-coming musicians in the Maritimes, then and now, saw his success as proof that even a Maritimer could achieve national and international success. You don't have to live in Toronto, New York, LA, or Nashville."

By 2009, Catherine MacLellan had come to terms with the famous family song and had begun singing it herself in concert, in a simple acoustic guitar version. "It took me a long time before I finally decided to learn 'Snowbird'. When I did, stripped down to its bare bones, it really is something. It breaks my heart, which is my favourite thing about any song. Technically, the melody touches on just about every note in the scale. The melody sweeps up and down and around in such a natural way; it really is a spectacular melody. And the lyrics — everyone has felt that, the desire to run away from things when you have a broken heart, not sure whether to stay or go, and just basic heartbreak.

"I've started playing it during shows, and it always gives me the chills. It is really a great song. I couldn't really hear it for what it was with all the Nashville strings and the sped-up tempo, but playing it myself I have really started to understand it and take it on myself. The imagery is so lovely, and, again, I just love heartbreak songs. To know that my dad wrote this and touched so many people's hearts with it is awe-inspiring. And now I have set myself a goal, to be even a quarter as good a songwriter as my father. I'm following in his footsteps, and it is a grand tradition to carry on. I hope he would be proud of me."

Bubbles

Actor, philosopher, musician, bar owner, cat whisperer, and cart-fixer, Bubbles is entertainment royalty in Canada. He serves as muse to some of the great musicians of our day, and has worked in close collaboration with Rush, The Tragically Hip, Guns N' Roses, Snow, George Canyon, and Sandbox. His life has been chronicled in touching detail on the sensitive and thought-provoking TV series *Trailer Park Boys*, and his on-screen charisma has led to a major motion picture career, including 2009's *Countdown To Liquor Day*. Denny Doherty, a fellow Haligonian and founding member of The Mamas and the Papas, once referred to Bubbles as "that weird guy with the glasses I had to get a restraining order on."

1. **LIMELIGHT – Rush**
It was a toss-up between this and "Closer To The Heart", but the guitar riff at the start of this one makes my bird point straight up!!!

2. **MONDAY, MONDAY – The Mamas and the Papas**
One of the greatest voices ever! And from just outside Sunnyvale Trailer Park!! God Love Denny!

3. **CINNAMON GIRL – Neil Young**
I'm not sure what a cinnamon girl is, but I love ladies and I love a big dirty warm cinnamon roll in the morning so . . .

4. **THESE EYES – The Guess Who**
I like blinking along to the piano part of this one.

5. **LOOKING FOR A PLACE TO HAPPEN – The Tragically Hip**
I like to think Gord wrote this about my kitties sizing up the litter box.

6. **INFORMER – Snow**
A salmonella-poisoned can o' nails — a leaky boom boom down!

7. **THE WRECK OF THE EDMUND FITZGERALD – Gordon Lightfoot**
I won't get on a fucking boat to this day

because of this one. Terrifying!

8. **BIG LEAGUE – Tom Cochrane & Red Rider**
This was all I listened to when I was writing letters to NASA trying to become a spaceman.

9. **SAY HELLO – April Wine**
This is one of the best songs out there for doing dirty stuff to.

10. **SNOWBIRD – Anne Murray**
You get this when you're tobogganing — if the bottom zipper of your snowsuit isn't done up tight!!

11 Big Yellow Taxi

Joni Mitchell

Reprise, 1970

Every so often, a pop song helps create a catchphrase. Few have stood the test time as much as the crucial line from "Big Yellow Taxi": "they paved paradise and put up a parking lot." Every time a green space gets developed or an old building is hauled down, somebody's going to repeat that lyric.

The song has stayed a surprising favourite for Joni Mitchell, too. She's been very careful about her back catalogue of hits over the years, especially as her music took a mid-career leap into jazz-influenced composition and she left her carefree folk days behind. She has made few concessions to her audience from the early days, but she has returned to "Big Yellow Taxi", embraced it, and even re-recorded a new version for 2007's *Shine* album.

Mitchell has treated the song differently in her recorded interpretations. The original, on *Ladies Of The Canyon*, is a swinging version, with doo-wop backing vocals and a silly ending, even a giggle. Despite the predictions of nature disappearing, DDT killing the wildlife, and trees having to be seen in museums, Mitchell and most of the hippie generation were still just as interested in groovin' as in saving the environment.

Mitchell's next recorded version was live, at an October 16, 1970, concert in Vancouver to benefit the new Greenpeace organization, which wanted help to send a boat to Alaska's Amchitka Island to protest a hydrogen bomb test. The song was certainly fitting for the occasion, yet once again Mitchell plays up the light-hearted angle, picking up the 1950s rock and roll vibe by segueing into the Larry Williams classic, "Bony Moronie", no doubt one of the dance-crazy teenaged Mitchell's favourite songs of the day.

By 1974, the song had become a full on rocker for the tour promoting her smash *Court And Spark* album. The former folkie was now leading a crack band of smooth jazz players, The LA Express, and here the song kicks along with a driving bass, duelling guitar and electric piano lines, a sax solo, and a new funk feel. This live version actually became the bigger US chart hit for Mitchell, cracking the Top Forty, unlike the original 1970 version, which had been a failure there; in Canada, though, the earlier version had been a bona fide Top Twenty hit.

By 2007, Mitchell's words, then nearly forty years old, seemed prophetic. For the *Shine* album, with its other songs tackling the degradation of the planet, "Big Yellow Taxi" fits in perfectly. The only update to the lyric she made was to change the price of admission to the tree museum from a buck and a half to an arm and a leg. And certainly this version is the most bittersweet: Mitchell no longer worries about the future; instead, she's living with the results. You can't say she didn't warn us.

12 Tom Sawyer

Rush
Mercury, 1981

My teenaged sons don't really know anything about radio stations, the Top Forty charts, hit singles, or new videos. They don't know what album a song is from or what other hits a band may have had. All they know about, or care about, is if the song is on a video game such as RockBand or Guitar Hero. That's their radio station. A thirty-year-old song is a brand-new hit to them the minute they discover it on a game.

So those three boys think Rush are about the biggest group in the world. Their favourite song is "Tom Sawyer", and that doesn't surprise drummer/ lyricist Neil Peart. "Yes, 'Tom Sawyer' remains probably our most popular song," he confirms, "in concert, in requests for use in movies such as *Waterboy*, *Small Soldiers*, *Fanboys*, *Adventures Of Power*, TV shows like *Family Guy*, *Chuck*, *The Colbert Report*, *Ellen* (yes really!), even the finale of *The Sopranos*, video games, and in steady airplay on classic rock radio."

The song came out of a session with another of Canada's favourite groups. "'Tom Sawyer' actually began with Rush playing on a Max Webster recording," says Peart, "a song called 'Battlescar'. Both complete bands crowded into a Toronto studio to play and sing on that track, and that day Max's lyricist, Pye Dubois, gave me an exercise book containing some of his lyrical ideas. The suggestion had been mine, for I had long admired Pye's lyrics for Max, and I always enjoy the process of collaboration (one reason I remain in the same band after almost thirty-five years). When I browsed through Pye's handwritten verses, I responded right away to the 'today's Tom Sawyer' idea. It contained Pye's usual vivid, gritty, streetwise imagery — surely his métier: when Max Webster was opening for Rush in the late seventies, how American audiences would roar when Kim [Mitchell] sang the line, 'Cocaine coloured computer cards' — and his clever wordplay."

Partly inspired by their friends in Max, Peart says the group entered a new writing phase: "Starting with the previous album, *Permanent Waves*, we had been experimenting with a more concise style of songwriting and, particularly, arranging. Nothing simple, of course, as we were still wedded to the challenges and rewards of complexity — and there is certainly a measure of that complexity in 'Tom Sawyer' that is well outside of what was generally considered 'radio-friendly,' even then. But as the three of us have often pointed out, a major motivator in our music has always been the quaint notion that it should be 'fun to play.' (The often-overlooked original seed of progressive rock, really: music that's fun to play!) If fun to play is combined with fun to listen to, you've got something special, and 'Tom Sawyer' is apparently a fair example of that. After almost thirty years, not only does that song remain popular with our fans, but after playing it hundreds, perhaps thousands, of times, it is still challenging and satisfying for us to perform it well."

13 Try

Blue Rodeo
Risque Disque, 1987

> "There are bands who had huge careers in Canada, and made their home and native land their artistic and commercial bread and butter. The poster child is Blue Rodeo."
>
> — Wilfred Langmaid, *The Daily Gleaner*

For ten years, all Greg Keelor and Jim Cuddy could do was try. Friends since high school, the duo paid their dues in the unheralded group The HiFis. They gave up on Toronto in the early eighties, headed for New York, and became Fly To France. Their fortunes weren't better there, so it was time to come home.

"'Try' was written at the end of our stay in New York, a kind of R&B song," remembers Jim Cuddy. "It was much faster, and it really kind of sucked, and I knew that. We decided we were done with all attachments to the current music. We were going to take Gordon Lightfoot's greatest hits, *Gord's Gold*, as our template and just strum the songs together. We took 'Try', which we thought was a good song and we put it into its simplest format, just slowed it down, and it was actually really nice."

The pair found Toronto more welcoming this time: "We didn't think it was that big a deal, but the song 'Try' got such a strong reaction. We played in the Horseshoe [Tavern], and we had to play it twice. People would make us do it again in the third set. We realized we had something, we didn't know what it was, but we knew we had a song that got people's attention."

Yet the song almost didn't get a chance to be heard. It was an album track on Blue Rodeo's debut disc, but they put out the title cut instead. "We didn't understand about singles, we didn't understand about ourselves," Cuddy realizes. "'Outskirts' did nothing. Then we put out 'Try', and it all of a sudden started getting radio play. I thought that's fantastic, and we were selling singles, selling records, but I didn't realize it was actually creating the platform for us to have a career. I didn't realize the power of radio."

"Try" crossed over to three different radio formats: Top Forty, country, and adult contemporary. "That's the kind of stuff we had no clue about, even while it was happening, even while we had all evidence of it. We'd go to places and they would be full. How did this happen? We just thought we were a live bar band."

The song was more than a hit. When people heard it, they became fans for life. Cuddy was worried the song was almost too big: "I took over a year off from singing it, it just got to me. For years in the bars, I was playing it twice a night. Then absolutely any performance anywhere, whether it was TV, radio, or live. Now I'm happy to do it, because I think people are looking at me thinking that I'm too old to hit the high notes. Maybe I was also thinking that was the only reason people liked us."

As you'll read later in the book, though, there would be plenty of other reasons people liked them.

14 New Orleans Is Sinking

The Tragically Hip
MCA, 1989

"Nothing else will make a room of thirty-somethings sing along like their lives depended on it."

— Leitha Haysom, CKBW

Canadian references, from place names to painters, can be found scattered across The Tragically Hip's songs throughout the band's career. They're dropped like seeds, with their young audience perhaps hearing the names Tom Thomson or Bobcaygeon for the first time. It seems incongruous, then, that the group's most popular song is set in the United States.

It actually refers to a very Canadian pastime, the road trip to the States. It happened to Gord Downie, the group's singer and lyricist, in the days before the band. "I went there with some great friends on a spur-a-the-moment trip," Downie writes in response to questions for this book. "We were committed. One of us declared, jumping into the back seat at a night time USA Truck Stop with a carton of smokes, that he, now, officially, had no money. We'd read the books, we'd seen the films. We understood what it meant to be young and in New Orleans at the tail end of Mardi Gras. And, of course, we understood nothing and it

was glorious. I feel these feelings when we play this song."

To appreciate the song, put yourself in that car of young Canadians, wide-eyed in that exotic city. "You can hear it in the very pronunciation of the name," explains Downie. "'New Or-leens' . . . Everything the song wants to say is in that pronunciation." It has remained the number one choice of fans, and by a large margin, despite the unending march of hits the group have presented. Not that Downie pays much attention to such things: "I don't think I did realize it. I do know we've played it almost every show since."

No matter how often the group play it, though, it's almost never the same. Downie has used the middle of the song to go into extended tall stories, making them up as he goes — anything from killer whales attacking him to murder-suicides — or he's incorporated lyrics from other songs and writers. For Downie, it's an ever-changing piece of performance art. "Really, every time we do any song

live, it's just another chance to edit, to 'go at it,' to add and subtract meaning, to improve and degrade the message, to keep the feeling of the song . . . alive and present. Presently, I've been screwing with the original version: 'Pale as a light bulb hanging on your wire / I was sucking onto something just to get a little higher / I was picking out the highlights of your scenery / I saw a little cloud, looked a little like me / I had my hands in your river / I had my knees along your banks / I looked up into your dark eyes above and immediately regretted saying thanks' . . . etc."

Of course, by the next time you see them live, you'll get a whole different version of "New Orleans Is Sinking". If you're a Tragically Hip fan, it'll no doubt still be the highlight of the show.

15 The Wreck Of The Edmund Fitzgerald

Gordon Lightfoot
MCA, 1989

"Not only haunting but respectfully poignant."

— Jaimie Vernon, *The Canadian Pop Music Encyclopedia*

Gordon Lightfoot isn't sure what made him write a song about a shipping disaster on Lake Superior, but he does remember clearly where he was on November 10, 1975: "I was working at home, at the kitchen table, and it came on the television, at eleven o'clock at night, the night it happened. But I didn't write the song until January. In doing so, I tried to get as much information as I could. I got an article out of *Newsweek* magazine and I got the newspapers. That's all we had back in those days; there were no computers, so you had to check the newspapers, get the chronology correct. It was done at the same time I was working on a whole bunch of other songs. It got done really fast, it got done by March, and the record came out in May or June of that year."

It quickly became much more than a song. The fame of the hit meant Lightfoot soon became connected with the families left behind. "The *Edmund Fitzgerald* has been a real experience for me. I've got to meet all the people, most of the relatives of all those guys. They're all still at the bottom of Lake Superior, in 550 feet of water. They'll never be able to recover any of them. I got to be involved, and I've done so willingly, and still am, with the aftermath of that event. It was to be expected of me to remain involved. I remember we had one event where we had over eight hundred people directly related, where they all got together, a great big reunion."

Lightfoot says family members have appreciated how he handled the story: "They all love the song, the song doesn't ask questions, it doesn't point fingers, it doesn't put blame on anybody like so many of those things do. It's just a nice recounting of the story. I think I succeeded in doing that quite well. I've never heard anything adverse. I wondered at the time if I would, but in a way, I knew that I wouldn't because I knew I had done it in what I thought was a proper manner." In 2010, a new documentary presented findings that blamed the sinking on a rogue wave, instead of human error. Lightfoot then announced he would start singing a new lyric, changing the line "the main hatchway gave in" to "caved in."

He has stayed involved to this day, serving as a fundraiser for scholarships, a friend, and a guardian of the rights to the story. "There's a ladies' committee in Madison, Wisconsin, that I refer all the requests to and we have to evaluate things. Like the time they were going to do a Hollywood movie on it. They didn't want that done, and neither did I. They've been my contact people, and they stay in contact with all the others.

"I try to put back. In many ways, their misfortune was my good fortune, because look at my success and career. So I've always tried to put back and cooperate, and be kind and be gentle, and be everything I can to these people."

16 Suzanne

Leonard Cohen
Columbia, 1967

"Brought poetry to the forefront of Canadian music."
— Ellen Mably, lyricist, Calgary

Bob Dylan opened many doors in the 1960s, and no one more surprising or talented came strolling in than Leonard Cohen. Already a literary star in Canada, the poet and novelist had reached a career crossroads by 1966. He was broke, and poetry wasn't paying the bills. Cohen had been living in Greece, had returned to Montreal, and was thinking about heading to Nashville, since he was once in a country-and-western band. But then he found out about Dylan, hailed as a poet, at least in popular music circles. Nashville was out, and New York was the new plan.

Cohen set some of his poems to music, including one called "Suzanne Takes You Down". Folk singer Judy Collins was his first major supporter, and had a hit with "Suzanne" in 1966, before Cohen recorded his own version.

Although both Cohen and the song's real-life muse, friend Suzanne Verdal of Montreal, insist their relationship was platonic, Cohen's reputation as the ultimate ladies' man began here and

has never abated. His long-time friend, vocalist, and co-writer Jennifer Warnes, was invited to share what "Suzanne", and Cohen, meant to her.

"I ran away from home seeking Jack Kerouac and found Leonard Cohen. I was unaware that before and after

"I hope it is true that a man can die and yet not only live in others, but give them life, and not only life, but that great consciousness of life."
— Jack Kerouac

this meeting, thousands of other free-spirited gypsy girls with similar agendas would pass through Leonard's life and he through theirs. 'Suzanne' was a real girl living in Montreal, before my time. Leonard admits that the 'tea and oranges' was actually [the tea brand] 'Constant Comment.'

"The sweet scenario described in 'Suzanne' was unfolding all over the world. It was an innocent and beautiful time. The love story is not new. But Leonard's vision was. His lyrics were elegant. Lesser writers became envious and mean-spirited toward Leonard. Songwriting can be a blood sport, full of competition.

"Decades after 'Suzanne', Leonard took me to Roy Orbison's wake where we shared a whiskey or tequila or something strong, acutely aware of how fragile our lives were. In a burst of tequila-fuelled urgency, I turned to my dear friend and whispered, 'Thanks for telling me the truth all these years. You didn't lie to me. I appreciate that. I suppose you didn't lie to those three thousand other women, either.' Leonard answered, 'Five thousand, Jenny'."

17 Life Is A Highway

Tom Cochrane
Capitol, 1991

"I was on the road with Tom when this song started to hit. It was a great experience watching the reaction to this tune getting crazier and crazier."

— Mike Campbell, manager, The Carleton

The period leading up to "Life Is A Highway" was emotional for Tom Cochrane. He was about to go solo. After years of recording with his group Red Rider, Cochrane was facing a split with his long-time music partner, steel guitar player Ken Greer. It wasn't an abrupt separation, but it had become obvious the two needed to go in different directions — very different, as it turned out. Greer hit the road with Gowan, while Cochrane went to Africa.

He'd become involved with the World Vision charity, and was asked to go to Mozambique, Ethiopia, and Somalia. Devastating famine was affecting tens of millions of people in these African nations. Back home, he did the interviews and spoke to his fans for the charity. The trip had left a deep mark on him. He described himself as mentally, physically, and spiritually exhausted at this time, and needed something to pull him out of a bleak mood.

Without Greer, Cochrane had begun to work on material on his own in his home studio. It was taking on a harder, more rhythm and blues edge. One number he'd had kicking around since the sessions for the 1984 *Breaking Curfew* album was a sketch called "Love Is A Highway". His mood still down, he woke in the middle of the night, inspired, and within a couple of hours, he'd changed the words and finished what would become his biggest hit. Instead of reflecting on the dire poverty he'd seen in Africa, Cochrane knew he needed something inspiring. It was his own cure, a refreshing, upbeat song that instantly changed his mood, and its positive energy was the key.

Instantly memorable, the song spread like a virus, with people singing its chorus and quoting the lyrics. Even David Letterman picked up on the lines, repeating them over and over for several nights. Inevitably, Cochrane appeared on the influential show, which helped push the song into the US Top 10 after it had already topped the Canadian charts. With the video of "Life Is A Highway", shot in Alberta's Badlands, Cochrane conquered all the media in 1991. The album that featured the song, *Mad Mad World*, reached diamond status in Canada, with more than one million copies sold. The single and the album also earned Cochrane four Juno awards.

Cochrane has continued his work for World Vision with more trips to Africa, as well as supporting other worthy causes in a long and distinguished career in charity work. He even teamed up with Greer a decade later, the Red Rider name proudly on display again. "Life Is A Highway" became a huge hit all over again in 2006 with a cover by Rascal Flatts from the movie *Cars*. And every time it comes on the radio, it still has that uplifting power, the musical cure Cochrane was searching for.

18 These Eyes

The Guess Who
Nimbus 9, 1969

"With Burton Cummings in the fold, they had the collective talent to be more than a one-hit wonder."

— Lee Marshall, broadcaster

Paying your dues — The Guess Who wrote the book on that one.

The band had spent the 1960s watching scores of other bands make hits while they barely stayed afloat. Even Winnipeg buddy Neil Young was now an unlikely pop star with Buffalo Springfield. But The Guess Who's career was a long series of near-misses and failed opportunities. The group had released a stunning fourteen singles since their last hit, 1965's "Shakin' All Over", and had even tried to latch onto Young's success by recording his "Flying On The Ground Is Wrong". But most Canadian radio stations had little use for the Prairie band.

Randy Bachman, however, was still working diligently to come up with the hit that would change everything and, since 1966, had pinned his hopes on the band's new singer, Burton Cummings. "Great ideas, great voice, and willing to try anything for a song," Bachman says of his partner. "Follow the rules and then break the rules. Write new rules. And use a different set of rules for every song written."

Bachman brought Cummings something he'd been toying with for a couple of months. "It came from the little piano intro I wrote. I also had the title 'These Arms', which became the second line of the song. It was a true collaboration in that I did the piano intro and some lyrics. He did lyrics and chords, and we both stumbled through a melody and wrote the song as a team."

The song got exposure on the CBC-TV show *Let's Go*, which featured The Guess Who as the house band from Winnipeg. Producer Jack Richardson believed in the band so much, he bought out their contract for $1,000 and set up a US record deal. The key would be getting a hit single in the States, since Canadian radio wasn't interested in them.

Everyone knew it should be "These Eyes", except the band. "Well, we liked the song," says Bachman, "but we didn't want a ballad released. We were a rock band and wanted to rock. Everyone above us thought it was the song to break us: Jack Richardson, the mixer; Phil Ramone, the head of RCA Records; Don Birkheimer; and people in radio. So that was the one."

The last piece of the puzzle was radio, and they finally found a champion at the most important station in Canada. "[Music director] Rosalie Trombley at CKLW in Windsor put it in high rotation. That station was a monster, and the keyhole for every band to get onto the airwaves of the USA. She and that station made the record, as her airplay spread to Detroit, Toledo, Cleveland, Buffalo, Chicago."

Randy Bachman, Jim Kale, and Garry Peterson had been recording together since 1962, and with Burton Cummings since 1966. They'd had their hopes dashed on failed trips to the United States and England, had lost all their money, but still had hope. "These Eyes" sold a million copies.

GORDON
LIGHTFOOT
Sundown
Demasiado tarde
para rezar

45-1096

reprise
RECORDS

19 Sundown

Gordon Lightfoot
Reprise, 1974

"There was no trust," says Gordon Lightfoot. "I was going with something, and the trust was not there, and I didn't know where she was at the time."

Like all of his songs, Gordon Lightfoot can tell you exactly what he was feeling at the time he wrote "Sundown". Like his previous smash, "If You Could Read My Mind", the song captures his emotional state shortly before a break-up. Straight out of the folk world, with songs celebrating pussy willows and Canadian railways, he had scored his two biggest hits by opening his heart. "It was just one of those miraculous things," he says. "Here I've got one about the marriage breaking up, and the next one's about somebody, perhaps, that I can't trust."

Lightfoot says that, for "Sundown", he picked up the guitar on a bad night. "I was writing at a farm out in the north end [of Toronto], I had moved out of my apartment, my marriage had broken up, I had a new girlfriend. We used to drive each other crazy, because we didn't have the complete trust that

couples should enjoy. I wrote that song directly as a result of that, on one night when I didn't really know where she was, for sure."

"Sundown" was a number one hit in North America. To get there, Lightfoot had made a big change to his sound, one that was still quite a move for a folk artist. "It had the beat," explains Lighfoot. "Those drums were added later. My band was John Stockfish [bass] and Red Shea [guitar], a wonderful little combo. It was just us doing a basic track with no drums on it. Nobody had any idea it might be a single right off the bat, but then it started to sound like a single." Producer Lenny Waronker filled out the sound, without Lightfoot knowing at first. "It didn't bother me none to add the drums. I was in good hands."

It was a career move Lightfoot had been planning since 1970's "If You Could Read My Mind": "I wanted the

follow-up. I wanted to keep this thing rolling. I wanted to get into doing bigger shows, perhaps add a couple of more musicians. Not necessarily go rock and roll. I've got lots of toe-tappers in my repertoire anyway, just as it stands. I wanted to be able to do it on my own terms, keep the folk idea into it.

"The whole album was really well played. I used to be able to listen to it

> "It was hard to choose the best song from him, but 'Sundown' has got a great groove to it."
> — Holly Thorne, Q92

on my eight-track stereo in my car, and I loved listening to it that way because it sounded so good. I remember one time I had my daughter in the car listening to it when she was only about ten years old, and she even commented to me how good it sounded, so that was all needed. I loved it, it was a good record, and it sold well, too."

20 Underwhelmed

Sloan
murderecords, 1992

"Prior to seeing the band for the first time, I sat in my Halifax hotel room listening to the CKDU sampler, which had 'Underwhelmed' on it. When the lyric changes from 'she rolled her eyes' to 'she rolled her R's' I knew my affection for the band had two big F's."

— Cam Carpenter, manager

"Underwhelmed" started it all for Sloan. It began with writer Chris Murphy, years before he even considered forming a modern rock band in Halifax.

Murphy talks us through the song's creation: "I know it was started at a time when I was writing poems, it was just like a free-form poem, it didn't rhyme at all. I would say it was 1987. So it was well before Sloan, which started in '91. I was playing with Andrew [Scott, drummer] in late 1990 or early '91 and I knew all the words, and I just made up a progression on the spot to make a tape for Patrick [Pentland, guitar player], who we were trying to get to join the band. Andrew and I just recorded it live on the spot, and I was making the melody on the spot. Glad we did, it paid off.

"We played it in our first show, which was February 1991 at the Nova Scotia College of Art and Design.

I think it was probably the first song we ever played. It's been through a couple of incarnations. When we first played it, it had sort of a tribal feeling. We recorded it that way on a little contest for the *Here And Now* compilation in September '91. The remixed version of that is on our *Peppermint* EP. By that time, we were in talks with [US label] Geffen. They were thinking of it as our big single, but we were already tired of it. We didn't want to put it on our *Smeared* record, and they basically were like, are you insane? So we ended up re-recording it, the sort-of Grunge version."

In concert over the years, it's been hard at times to tell if Murphy considers the song a highlight or a burden. To this day, audiences still yell for it, which at times has annoyed him mid-show. Shouted requests sometimes see him scold audiences. "That won't strengthen your case," he chuckles.

"To tell you the truth," he confides, "I haven't fallen out of love with it. I think it's great. I think it's too long, but it's all about the lyrics. It's just a repetitive riff, nothing really happens, but it's basically a folk song in that it's just a story, a little funny story. The hatred really is Andrew's — he's like, 'Jesus, don't make me play that,' and I don't have the heart to make him. But we don't do it a lot these days."

Still, Murphy understands why fans still consider this the group's high point. He says it's the same for almost every band. "You love their first record, or you love their first three, and then your love goes down from there. And judging by what I understand is the order of people's love of our songs, it started early and drops off around 1998," he laughs. "But I still care for the song, I think it's cute."

21 Up on Cripple Creek/The Night They Drove Old Dixie Down

The Band
Capitol, 1969

"Just a beautiful sound that is like the earth itself rising up to sing its song."
— Randy Gelling, CFUV

The Band's debut album, 1968's *Music From Big Pink*, had been hailed as an instant classic and immediately influenced leading musicians such as Eric Clapton and George Harrison. The group's sound and vision were based on a desire to ignore fashions and technology and instead concentrate on the roots of the music they loved. Suddenly, psychedelia and studio polish were old hat, and many of the world's top artists started focusing on musicianship and song craft.

For the follow-up album, simply called *The Band*, producer John Simon was back on board, once again serving as the sixth member of the group. He says there was no plan to make music that reflected the past instead of the present: "Not consciously, except for the fact that we made no effort to keep up with the Joneses. In contrast, Paul Simon, Steve Forbert, and others I've worked with were very aware of how their music fit in with current trends."

Instead of the usual image of The Band, tucked away in rural Woodstock in a funky pink house, these songs were recorded at Sammy Davis Jr.'s place. "Since the first album was a hit, we were indulged more," says Simon. "We rented a house in the Hollywood Hills and Capitol Records provided the recording equipment for us there. Also, as is the case with most second albums, there was no backlog of songs waiting to be recorded, so a lot of the writing took place there."

This double-sided single features two classic Southern-flavoured tales, as sung by Arkansas's Levon Helms. The first, "Up On Cripple Creek", stars a good ol' boy who wants to get back to his Louisiana belle. She's a free spirit, and the fun-loving performance fits the girl. Only a reference to comedian-bandleader Spike Jones puts a date on the song, but it could be anywhere from the Dirty Thirties to today. This tale, and others, came from the story swapping they enjoyed and the jam sessions that came after. "Robbie [Robertson] was generally the shot caller," says Simon, "because of his personality and the personalities of the others. However, if anyone else felt strongly about something, attention would be paid. We experimented a lot. Everyone pretty much made their own instrumental choices, Garth's [keyboardist Hudson] choices being the icing on the cake."

The flip side has become an iconic number, a Civil War story that evokes perfectly the sorrow of the South. Helms's plaintive vocal is matched by the mournful horns of Hudson and Simon. Although not a hit for the group, "Dixie" received significant FM airplay, and Joan Baez took the number into the charts. "Cripple Creek" did better in Canada than in the United States, becoming a Top Ten hit. But hits weren't the point; it was the music. Says Simon, "It was part of the atmosphere of the whole album. I wasn't thinking commercially — just artistically. I never have."

22 Let Your Backbone Slide

Maestro Fresh-Wes
Attic, 1989

> "It marked the emergence of rap culture into the Canadian mainstream."
>
> — Heidi Petracek, CBC-TV

Wes Williams became the most successful rap performer in Canada with "Let Your Backbone Slide". He did it by completely ignoring the usual medium for a hit single. "Well to be quite honest, I wasn't really stressing radio," says Maestro. "It was MuchMusic, that was the new form of getting your music out there, promoting yourself. It was visual. It was very important to get your video out there, that was the main, main thing in Canada: to be seen."

Much has been made about the trouble African Americans went through to gain video exposure, even after Michael Jackson's breakthrough on MTV. But Maestro says there was no similar colour barrier at Canada's MuchMusic. "No way, man! They were so accommodating it was ridiculous, man. They played my very first video, which was 'I'm Showin' You', a video that I paid for myself. Farley Flex's mother co-signed the loan for me. I put $2,000 of my own money into it, she co-signed the loan for three grand,

so it was a five-g video that I shot at my high school. I was smart enough to know back then that national exposure is a beautiful thing, regardless of the quality of the video. So MuchMusic, they gave it some spins, and the quality wasn't the greatest, but it was Canadian content, and I'm glad I was a part of it."

The title phrase for the hit came from an unlikely source, a piece of 1981 US hair metal. "I kept saying it, 'let your backbone slide,'" says Maestro. "I got inspired by Billy Squier. He did a song called 'The Stroke'. He said 'make my backbone slide,' and I was just like, wow, that's so hot. I was like, you know what, I'm gonna keep that, I'm gonna use that, make a song called 'Let Your Backbone Slide'. It sounded so cool, it was cool slang, that was so dope. It sounded so funky."

The single, and the album

Symphony In Effect, set sales records for rap that still haven't been beaten in Canada. While he's proud of that, Maestro says it's only because hip-hop has never fully been accepted here. "It's just because there's no industry here," says Maestro. "It isn't because there's a lack of talent. It's been twenty years now, man — these Canadian labels ain't got it. I just want an industry here, man. I'd just like to see more than one artist do well at the same time. Not one artist, then five years later another. I'm tired of having people look back at me, reference me, what I've done, back in the day. I wanna see people excel. I don't need to stroke my ego — that don't mean nothing to the kids coming up. I'm proud of what I've accomplished. It's just time to see people take it to the next level. It's two decades, man. It's not funny no more."

23 Tired Of Waking Up Tired

The Diodes
CBS, 1978

"Great punk song. Sum 41 should do this so The Diodes can finally get some royalties."

— Stephen Cooke, *The Chronicle Herald*

Toronto's Diodes led the way in Toronto's punk scene, responsible for importing the new style and attitude. "The Diodes formed in October 1976 at the Ontario College of Art," singer Paul Robinson recalls, "and played their first gig supporting Talking Heads in January 1977. There were no other punk bands playing in Toronto. John [Catto, guitar] had spent part of the summer [1976] hanging out with the New York Dolls who played Toronto. They were managed by Malcolm McLaren [later of Sex Pistols fame], and John was taken with his visual rock and roll eye. We went to NYC and bought clothes from a shop which carried gear from Mclaren's and Vivienne Westwood's SEX."

The Diodes became the first Canadian punk band on a major label. "The A&R guys from CBS Canada had been to their worldwide convention in June 1977," says Robinson. "They saw The Clash live, came back to Toronto and said, 'Boys, we have to find our own punk band.' In those days everything happened fast. We signed in late August, and recorded the album in the first two weeks in September. It was on the shelves by October, making it one of the earliest punk albums in the world, two months before The Sex Pistols' *Never Mind The Bollocks*."

The rest of it wasn't that easy. It was almost impossible to find a place to play. "We had a gig in the basement of a Yonge Street bar called The Colonial Underground," says Robinson. "We thought we had arrived. Everyone in the Toronto scene was there: The Curse, The Viletones, The B Girls, and Teenage Head. Unfortunately, Long John Baldry was upstairs playing, and the bouncers were sent to shut us down. They grabbed pool cues and were extremely aggressive to everyone. First they cut the PA, and then all hell broke loose. We had only played three songs. It ended in a riot with several people needing hospital treatment. From this point, no one would book any of the Toronto punk bands."

So they created their own club, the now legendary Crash 'n' Burn. "We were given the keys to the basement of the Centre for Experimental Art and Communication for the summer to rehearse while the owners were in Europe. We soon saw the opportunity to open it on weekends. All of the original Toronto punk bands were given a slot as support for bands we booked from NYC and LA, including The Nerves, The Dead Boys, The Dishes, The Poles, The Dents. Some of the Ramones even got up and jammed."

By connecting Toronto to the rest of the booming punk world, The Diodes opened up connections for their own songs. "Tired Of Waking Up Tired" has consistently impressed successive generations of punk and power pop fans. "I think it has one of the best chorus hooks of any songs written during this period," says Robinson, "but perhaps I'm just a bit biased."

THE TOP 100 FRENCH-CANADIAN SINGLES

As mentioned in the introduction to this book, French-speaking Canadians have enjoyed a vibrant and successful recording scene for decades. French Canada features its own hits, stars, and styles, and hit albums and singles have regularly sold hundreds of thousands of copies — impressive numbers compared with sales figures from English Canada. It can be argued that homegrown music plays a more important role in the lives of francophones than it does for anglophones. Since most English-speaking Canadians don't hear this music, it's impossible to create a truly definitive list that covers both French and English hits. French-speaking Canadians deserve their own Top 100, so I've separated the votes and created a list that features the top French vote-getters among the thousands of songs suggested by the panel of jurors. I hope anglophone readers use the list as an introduction to these excellent Canadian artists.

ROBERT CHARLEBOIS

MALAJUBE

1. **Robert Charlebois – Lindberg**
2. **Malajube – Montréal -40°**
3. **Harmonium – Pour un instant**
4. **Jean Leloup – 1990**
5. **Jean-Pierre Ferland – Le petit roi**
6. **Gilles Vigneault – Mon pays**
7. **Beau Dommage – La complainte du phoque en Alaska**
8. **Félix Leclerc – Le p'tit bonheur**
9. **Raymond Lévesque – Quand les hommes vivront d'amour**
10. **Claude Dubois – Le blues du businessman**
11. Les Colocs – Tassez-vous de d'là
12. Robert Charlebois – Ordinaire
13. Michel Pagliaro – J'entends frapper
14. Daniel Bélanger – Opium
15. Richard Desjardins – Tu m'aimes-tu
16. Jean Leloup – Isabelle
17. Gilles Vigneault – Gens du pays
18. Céline Dion – Pour que tu m'aimes encore
19. Daniel Lavoie – Ils s'aiment

20. Gilles Valiquette – Je suis cool (asteur)
21. Harmonium – Un musicien parmi tant d'autres
22. Octobre – La maudite machine
23. Paul Piché – Heureux d'un printemps
24. Daniel Bélanger – Sèche tes pleurs
25. Mes Aïeux – Dégénérations/ Le reel du fossé
26. Mitsou – Bye bye mon cowboy
27. Diane Tell – Si j'étais un homme
28. Félix Leclerc – Le tour de l'île
29. Céline Dion – L'amour existe encore
30. Plume Latraverse – Bobépine
31. Nanette Workman – Ce soir on danse à Naziland
32. Beau Dommage – Harmonies du soir à Châteauguay
33. Harmonium – Harmonium
34. Jean-Pierre Ferland/Ginette Reno – Un peu plus haut, un peu plus loin
35. Robert Charlebois – Fu Man Chu
36. Jean Leloup – I Lost My Baby

37. Daniel Lanois – Jolie Louise
38. Daniel Boucher – La désise
39. Les Cowboys Fringants – Les étoiles filantes
40. Claude Gauthier – Le plus beau voyage
41. Xavier Caféïne – Montréal (cette ville)
42. Pierre Lapointe – Deux par deux rassemblés
43. Jean Leloup – Sang d'encre
44. Michel Rivard – Le retour de Don Quichotte

BEAU DOMMAGE

JEAN-PIERRE FERLAND

45. Jean-Pierre Ferland – La musique

46. Malajube – Étienne d'Août

47. Fabienne Thibeault – Le monde est stone

48. Daniel Bélanger – Rêver mieux

49. Paul Piché – L'escalier

50. Artistes variés (Star Académie) – Et c'est pas fini

51. Michel Rivard – Schefferville, le dernier train

52. Éric Lapointe – Mon ange

53. Félix Leclerc – L'alouette en colère

54. Les Trois Accords – Hawaienne

55. Kevin Parent – Seigneur

56. Offenbach – Promenade sur mars

57. Robert Charlebois – Entre deux joints

58. Beau Dommage – Montréal

59. Laurence Jalbert – Encore et encore

60. Harmonium – Comme un sage

61. Roch Voisine – Hélène

62. Les Cowboys Fringants – Plus rien

63. Robert Charlebois – Tout écartillé

64. Jean Leloup – Johnny Go

65. Ariane Moffatt – Point de mire

66. Claude Léveillée – Frédéric

67. Possession simple – Comme un cave

68. Natasha St-Pier – Je n'ai que mon âme

69. Céline Dion – Une colombe

70. Richard Séguin – Protest Song

71. Daniel Lavoie – Tension Attention

72. Claude Dubois – Plein de tendresse

73. Les B.B. – T'es dans la lune

74. Pagliaro – M'lady

75. Bruno Pelletier – Le temps des cathédrales

76. Les Colocs – La rue Principale

77. Marjo – Je sais, je sais

78. Raymond Lévesque – Bozo-les-culottes

79. Diane Juster – Je ne suis qu'une chanson

80. La Bolduc – Ça va venir, découragez-vous pas

81. Kevin Parent – Fréquenter l'oubli

82. Martine St'Clair – Ce soir l'amour est dans tes yeux

83. Serge Fiori/Richard Séguin – Viens danser

84. Jean Leloup – Edgar

85. Mario Pelchat – Je n't'aime plus

86. Coeur de Pirate – Ensemble

87. Claude Dubois – Si Dieu existe

88. Offenbach – J'ai l'rock 'n' roll pis toé

89. Harmonium – Dixie

90. Richard Séguin – Aux portes du matin

91. Karkwa – Oublie pas

92. Nicola Ciccone – J't'aime tout court

93. Ariane Moffatt – Je veux tout

94. Gerry Boulet – Un beau grand bateau

95. Marjo – Chats sauvages

96. Beau Dommage – Le blues d'la métropole

97. Céline Dion – Incognito

98. Diane Dufresne – Rock pour un gars de bicycle

99. Annie Blanchard – Évangéline

100. Malajube – Pâte Filo

24 The Spirit Of Radio

Rush
Mercury, 1980

While this book honours the single, it also serves to celebrate radio. That's where we heard many of these songs for the first time. Tuning in as a kid was a magic experience for Rush's Neil Peart.

"I thought the performers were actually there, at the radio station," he remembers. "I must have figured they travelled around from one radio station to another, singing their songs. That sounded like fun. Later, when I learned it was records that were played on the radio, introduced so effusively by these larger-than-life voice characters called disc jockeys, I had another illusion — that those disc jockeys were playing the music they liked, just because they wanted to."

As any disc jockey forced to play "You Light Up My Life" can tell you, they didn't have that freedom. They had a playlist and orders to stick to it. There had been a time, however, when such stations existed, in the late 1960s, when FM was starting.

For Peart, that was the spirit of radio. "As a young listener in the suburbs of a small Ontario town, radio was a friendly place, as expressed in the opening line of the song: 'Begin the day with a friendly voice.' Listening to your favourite radio station day and night, you got to know the quirky personalities of the FM jocks and the weird music they sometimes played. Those experiences, and those times, could only encourage a young idealist, because I could believe that some things were what they appeared to be. There seemed every reason to believe you could be part of that: make music you liked and have other people like it, too."

But radio had changed by the time Peart joined the music machine, and most FM stations now had playlists as well. There was one exception Peart knew of: "In the late seventies, there was a small independent just outside of Toronto that still clung to a remarkably loose format. One of their few strictures was that they wouldn't play the same song twice in one day, which is pretty cool in itself, and their slogan was 'the Spirit of Radio.' The on-air guys at CFNY really did seem to have the freedom to create interesting combinations of songs. I always think of driving over the Niagara Escarpment late one night, and Dave Marsden played a long sequence that began with 'Take Me to the River' by Talking

"Those days are long gone but the feeling is not."
— Kevin Hilliard, writer/musician

Heads, then the epic 'Dancing With The Moonlit Knight' by Genesis, and finally segued into our long instrumental, 'La Villa Strangiato', doubtless one of the few times that monster was ever played on radio! So, 'The Spirit of Radio' was partly a celebration of how great that station could be — how great radio could be — of the simple joy of driving along and listening to the radio, and partly an angry protest at what commercial radio had become."

25 Oh What A Feeling

Crowbar
Daffodil, 1971

Call it the Spirit of '69. The events of that heady year inspired Crowbar's Kelly Jay to write the band's great anthem. "The whole deal about 1969 was that my daughter was born," says Jay, starting his list. "Man walked on the moon, there was Woodstock, so many positive things that happened then. These things were so important. They were world shaking. It was 9/11 in reverse, we were so hopeful."

That was the feeling Jay was talking about, that was the rush. "We thought we were the kings of the world," he laughs. "We were living in a mansion, Bad Manors, on twenty-five acres in the Hammer [Hamilton]. We were friends with John Lennon and Yoko Ono. We had some pretty amazing parties. Kris Kristofferson, The Guess Who, all the bands, there was a lot of really amazing people. We felt we were something unique."

It took a couple of years to get the song out to the public, but the timing couldn't have been better. The contentious Canadian content regulations had just been introduced, forcing radio stations to play more Canadian songs. "Oh What A Feeling" is considered the first-ever CanCon hit. The man behind the regulations, CRTC chairman Pierre Juneau, praised the band for proving Canadians could make just as great music as the big US and British bands. "Juneau thanked me on stage one night at the Junos," says Jay, "and my mother and father saw it, and, oh my God, they were thrilled."

> **"The authentic party atmosphere sums up the time."**
>
> — Ric Taylor, writer-broadcaster

It became the band's signature song, and even provided the secret password to let you into the band's inner circle, from the nonsense lyrics in the hook. "That's what it's known as to the band, 'ba-ba-da-ba,' and if you say that to anybody in the band, they know what you're talking about," reveals Jay. "All kinds of people would come up to Bad Manors, and if you knew it you were in the door. Or we used to refer to us going to play, we're going 'ba-ba-da-bah.' Tiffany, my daughter, who was growing up in Bad Manors, a five-year-old kid, that's what she'd say, 'Daddy going ba-ba-da-ba?'"

Jay and the rest of the members are widely regarded as one of the most exciting and talented groups to ever perform in the country. They were never able to repeat the huge success of "Oh What A Feeling", but Jay is justifiably proud of the song and of the group's career. "I've heard it cracked that we're the original one-hit wonder. I don't feel like we're a one-hit wonder, but I do feel like we had a diamond to put on the top of our crown. And it doesn't matter — one hit, ten hits — I never claimed we were The Beatles, but we sure had a lot of fun."

He has one last piece of wisdom for those searching fame and fortune in rock music: "I've been in the music business for almost fifty years and I've made hundreds and hundreds of dollars."

26 High School Confidential
Rough Trade
True North, 1981

"Can't believe this scandalous song made it to the mainstream."
— Jelena Adzic, CBC-TV

It was a boy-meets-girl love story, set in the hippie days of the 1960s. No, seriously, that's the start of Rough Trade.

"Carole [Pope] and I met in Toronto, 1968, Yorkville," confirms Kevan Staples. "We met at an audition for singers for my band. My whole life changed that day. I fell in love right away because she was so unusual. She was incredibly shy. She wrote these unusual songs with unusual choices of words. I thought, who is this girl? She was just so fascinating. So we became, instantly, boyfriend-girlfriend."

By the late 1970s, that shy girl had changed a bit, and the duo was causing a stir, a bit too much for some in still-conservative Toronto. "Record companies always had a hard time with us," Staples says. "Not that they didn't get it, they were afraid of us. It still was sort of the dawn of the feminist movement, and a lot of people didn't want to deal with a woman who had what Carole had to say. It was the content, too much social-sexual politics and feminist viewpoints."

The duo came up with a song so strong, yet still provocative, that the music establishment caved in. "High School Confidential" was originally written for the 1980 Al Pacino movie *Cruising*. "Carole wrote the lyrics from a guy's standpoint," says Staples. "We wrote about eight songs, and they only used a couple in the movie, so we did it as one of our songs. It takes on a different complexion by having a woman singing it."

Rough Trade handed radio a phrase never heard in pop music before: "They had a hard time with 'cream my jeans.' We weren't trying to be shocking or provocative, that wasn't our intention. To us, it was social satire, sexual politics, and social commentary. We certainly didn't think about it when we were writing it. We didn't go 'oh boy, this is going to stir up a hornet's nest.' It was just the act of being yourself. For us, it was just amusing. Radio wouldn't play it until we did an edited version. We tried changing the lyrics to something funny, and then we

just decided, forget it, we'll just bleep it. We were so stupid, but it just got it more press, and any press is good press. So it got more attention from that."

The song's legacy has become a pleasant surprise for Staples. "Many years later people came up to us and said, 'When I was fourteen or fifteen and I played that song, it meant so much to me as a gay person who was not yet out.' And I found that fascinating. There was this huge demographic of young kids, both male and female, who that song really spoke to, even though that certainly wasn't what we were aiming for when we wrote it. Somehow it became an anthem for the quiet gay community. Which was really nice."

27 Echo Beach
Martha & The Muffins
Dindisc, 1979

ECHO BEACH
(M. Gane)
From the Virgin Din Disc Album
"METRO MUSIC" V 2142
Prod: Mike Howlett

Virgin

SIDE ONE
Stereo

-dindisc

VS 1111
(VS 1111-AS)
Time: 3:38

MARTHA & THE MUFFINS
Nymph Music,
Inc. (BMI)
℗ 1980 Dinsong Limited

"A blast of pure pop energy."
— Grant Kerr, music writer

Let's get this out of the way right now: where's Echo Beach?

"I didn't really have any concrete place, it was just a place in the mind," says songwriter Mark Gane. "Subsequently, of course, people from all over the world were going, there's an Echo Beach here, that must be the one. We got lots of letters from people that claimed that their Echo Beach was the one and, of course, it is the one. Everybody's got one, that's their beach."

The idea of getting away from it all and escaping to your own private paradise appealed to an audience worldwide. "My father was talking to me once about it," says Gane, "and said, 'Do you know why it's so big? It's because it taps into nostalgia, but it's modern at the same time.' I think that's right, because it refers to a place you've been, and there's a longing there, and it's universal. The only line that I can remember being deliberate about was 'My job is very boring, I'm an office clerk.' I got the idea for this song when I was working in a wallpaper factory, and I thought, I can't say, 'My job is very boring, I work in a wallpaper factory.' So that's when I went, what could be a really tedious job? It had something to do with [singer] Martha Johnson, who had a really boring clerical job at the Ontario Health Insurance Plan."

Canadian record labels weren't interested in the band and their modern, odd sound. However, England knew their New Wave, and the group were signed to the powerhouse Virgin label. "That's where it broke," says Gane. "The British press had never seen a band like ours. It's hard to imagine now, but we were greeted with great curiosity because Canada was considered a wasteland, with folk singers and outdated heavy metal stuff. Even back then you were getting this surprised condescension — like, who's this weird band from the colonies? Once it was doing well in the UK, then Europe, Australia, and everywhere else, then Canada was into it as well.

I think, given the times, it would never have happened if it had come out of Canada."

The appeal of the song, thirty years later, is staggering. "We have a Google alert set to 'Echo Beach', so every day, somewhere around the world, something's happening with that song. There's a science fiction story based on it, there's a gay porno film, there was a dance club in San Francisco, there's a clothing line, there's a famous stretch of beach in Orange County, there's an Irish horse-jumping champion, there's an iris named after it. There's a TV series in the UK, there's a youth hostel in Australia, there are hotels in Zanzibar and Bali, and they're all based on the song. It's bizarre. It astounds me, and as a songwriter, it's extremely gratifying."

28 Sweet City Woman

The Stampeders
MWC, 1971

"It makes me think of how unique and pure music sounded to me in the early 1970s."

— Dan Reynish, CBC Radio

"Sweet City Woman" starts like no other song on pop radio, then or now. It still jumps out at you, it's unmistakable and instantly recognizable. It's the banjo.

Rich Dodson wrote the song shortly after the group moved to Toronto from their birthplace, Calgary. "I wrote it in Toronto, end of '70 into '71. I guess just coming down from Calgary, playing down east, into Montreal. It was just a summation of us coming down from out west, doing our country-rock thing into the city of Toronto, a meld of all those things. I guess the lick came to me, a funky lick, and we put it together and started playing it at gigs, and got really good reaction to it."

There was still one important piece missing in the song, though, and it came to Dodson in a stroke of luck: "On the way to the studio, I thought the lick might be really cool with a banjo, so I rented one at Long & McQuade and used it on the session.

It really worked. It was the right thing."

At first, there were warnings you couldn't put a banjo on a pop single. "That was the reaction of the record company," remembers Dodson. "No way is anybody going to play a banjo in top pop radio, but it just took off like a rocket. CHUM-AM was the big station. They couldn't believe the phone calls and the reaction. They actually had to send somebody down from the radio station to A&A and Sam The Record Man, 'cause they didn't believe it was selling that well. So they sent their own spies down to the record stores to count the bins. This was when Canadian records weren't really getting played, weren't getting much reaction, and weren't really taken seriously. So it was justified — we were selling better than everybody, McCartney and the works, and it went number one and they couldn't stop it."

Despite the move to Toronto,

everybody still thought the band were from Calgary, thanks to the name. It turns out the group never liked or wanted to be The Stampeders. "We had an investor that wanted us to use that name, but we weren't that keen on it," admits Dodson. "And he never came up with the cash. But when we started getting responses from Europe and South America, and they all think it's the neatest thing, you say, hmm, maybe we'll hold on to that, just leave it alone. This is so bad, it's good."

The Stampeders had a string of hits throughout the seventies. But what happened to the fourth member of the group, the real star of "Sweet City Woman"? After the session, the banjo went back to its owners. "Long & McQuade say they sold that banjo five thousand times," says Dodson, as bands rushed to the store to grab some of that magic. "That's the one! Somebody out there's got it."

29 Wake Up

Arcade Fire
Merge, 2004

> "It's an arena rock song written for people who just like good music."
>
> — Meghan Gamble, Open Road Recordings

Arcade Fire came together in a unique way, fuelled by love and family. Texas-born Win Butler had moved to Montreal in 2000 to go to McGill University, and fell in love with the city, its music scene, and Régine Chassagne, who joined the band. Members came and went, but by 2003, Win needed more support. That's when his brother Will crossed the border. "I moved to Montreal for six months during my sophomore year of college," says Will. "I took off the spring trimester and stayed through the summer. Those six months were sort of the birth of [debut album] *Funeral*. The new lineup of the band was coming together. It was not necessarily fun — we didn't really have a drummer for the six months I was there."

What they had was an exciting sound. The members were all multi-instrumentalists, and brought that freedom into the studio. It was solid modern rock, and the group was unafraid to bring in synths, strings, massed choral vocals and chants, women and men in equal roles, fine melodies, and old-fashioned power chords. That's the musical recipe behind "Wake Up", the most-loved track from *Funeral*.

"'Wake Up' was one of the first songs the new lineup tackled," says Will. "Originally the first section was quieter — sort of a more Chinese orchestra section, less of a Scottish war chant. I think Tim [Kingsbury] and I made it a little more balls-out rock and roll, for better or worse. The balls-to-the-wall nature of the song was really cemented the first couple of times we played live — when everyone's singing and the drums are loudly playing 'We Will Rock You' [the Queen hit], and the place you're playing in is tiny and holds maybe a hundred people tops, the song comes off much more as a 'Hey, asshole, try to ignore this,' and much less as a life-affirming anthem."

While the album eventually became a success, it was the live shows that brought the group its exciting reputation, especially an appearance at New York's "Fashion Rocks" show in 2005, with David Bowie joining them for "Wake Up". The song became a YouTube essential.

"I loved playing 'Wake Up' on those first tours," says Will Butler, "when nobody had heard our songs and nobody knew anything about us. We played a show in Brantford, Ontario, where we took up more than 50 per cent of the room. There were maybe eighteen kids packed around the walls, and we still did the full show as loud as we could play it. Those songs were really fun to shove in people's faces. The first rule is you have to be memorable. Then worry about being good, then meaningful. I think hearing 'Wake Up' for the first time in a live show in a tiny venue would be very memorable — only three chords, [an] easy melody, and it's pretty well crammed down your throat by the people on stage."

30 If I Had $1000000

Barenaked Ladies
Independent, 1991

Although "If I Had $1000000" had been around since 1988, the version most Canadians heard came from the group's smash hit cassette, *The Yellow Tape*. It was also the beginning of a very fruitful partnership for the co-singers and songwriters in the band, childhood friends Steven Page and Ed Robertson. "It may have been our first song we wrote together," reflects Page. "We'd known each other since grade school. We were working together at this music camp in 1988. I was just eighteen, and he learned a bunch of songs I had written. At that same camp, he started entertaining the kids with this song he had written off the top of his head. When he got home, he said, 'I gotta play you this song,' and I just started doing the answer lines right back. That was the nature of our relationship — we were always able to finish each other's sentences."

It became the group's signature song, with Robertson and Page making up new parts on stage. "It took on a life of its own," says Page. "We'd do twenty-minute versions. We're bantering, we're throwing other songs

in there, we'd even do an operatic version." The song's humour was a key part of the group's early success, bringing laughter back into rock at a time when it was too serious. They sang about K-cars, bad furniture, and Kraft Dinner. "It was part of our thing, examining life as we knew it, in the late eighties," Page explains. "It was our culture, but nobody was talking about it. At that time, everything was so earnest, all the bands were like U2. But we knew these other bands were just like us, from the same backgrounds. So it was us poking fun at that seriousness."

Page remembers when he realized he'd co-written a Canadian classic: "In 1993, we were on our tour, and I got laryngitis and ended up in hospital in PEI. We had to cancel a show, and I went down for a smoke and there was an elderly woman with an oxygen

> "There is no other song so deeply entrenched in the Canadian consciousness as this silly bit of fluff."
> — Melissa Martin, music journalist

mask, and she said, 'I heard you're a musician, do you play "Achy Breaky Heart"? No? Do you play "Million Dollars"? That's when I knew we were part of the consciousness. To know that you've written a song that every Canadian knows, it's pretty amazing."

Page believes the band took it for granted. "We never gave it the respect it deserved until much later. Our first hit in Toronto was 'Be My Yoko Ono', a lesser song I think, and then other songs took precedent, like 'One Week'. I love 'If I Had $1000000'. It's one of the only BNL songs that I sang that I don't do now in my solo show. I don't have a problem doing 'Brian Wilson' or whatever. But of all the songs, it's the one that is totally me and Ed. I have a lot of respect for it, and I'd hate to mess with it for people."

31 Lindberg

Robert Charlebois avec Louise Forestier
Gamma, 1968

"Charlebois was Quebec rock's poet master. This is his finest moment."
— Larry Leblanc, *The Leblanc Newsletter*

Robert Charlebois can be considered the single most important figure in modern Quebec pop music. With his landmark album *Robert Charlebois/ Louise Forestier*, he dramatically ushered in the sound of rock and roll mixed with the more traditional singer-songwriter material of the *chansonnier*. The key song was the huge Quebec hit "Lindberg".

Charlebois' first three albums featured the normal acoustic guitar strumming of the *chanson*. Then a trip to California right in the middle of the 1967's "Summer of Love" triggered a transformative career rebirth. He soaked up the psychedelic influences, and came back to Quebec with fresh ideas.

Louise Forestier was following a similar path. A young trained actress, she had recently come to provincial fame with folk music albums and been named Radio-Canada's discovery of the year. She joined Charlebois' circle of musicians, actors, and poets, and on his new, groundbreaking album, she became the perfect vocal partner for his transition to harder rock.

Charlebois was the first *chansonnier* to use electric guitar on his songs. The backing leapt from folk to rock to jazz, all with a theatrical flair, featuring the free jazz of Quatuor du Jazz Libre du Québec. For the lyrics, he teamed with young poets Claude Péloquin and Marcel Sabourin. Their sometimes surreal and psychedelic stories were told in the language of working-class Quebecers, using slang and modern phrases and a bit of English, the same way anyone on the streets of Montreal would speak.

On stage, there was also a major transformation. Charlebois now played the part of a rock star, wearing wild costumes, screaming and swearing, blasting out psychedelic and hard rock, pretty much creating a spectacle by using his theatrical past. All the old, staid rules of the formal *chansonnier* were forgotten, and every Quebec rock musician to follow felt Charlebois' influence.

"Lindberg" featured a lyric from Péloquin, and hit like a blast on Quebec radio. It's a flight of fancy, based around the true story of famed aviator Charles Lindbergh's visit to Quebec City in 1928. Instead of Lindbergh's *Spirit of St. Louis*, the airplane in the song is jokingly called the "Holy Spirit of Duplessis," after the Quebec premier. The song starts slowly and strumming, with Charlebois and Forestier weaving their voices around each other in a full duet. Then the band kick in after the first chorus. The singers become more dramatic and forceful as the drums drive them on, the dreamy duet becoming a theatrical rocker. Forestier at times imitates a cross between a trumpet and a police siren. The lyrics, provocative humour, and wild backing made the song a mind trip, and ushered Quebec music into the psychedelic era. Forestier and Charlebois became the province's own Grace Slick and Marty Balin (of Jefferson Airplane). Almost overnight, pop music changed for good in Quebec.

32 I'm An Adult Now
The Pursuit Of Happiness
TPOH, 1986

Nothing speaks more to the power of video and MuchMusic in the mid-eighties than the success of "I'm An Adult Now". Transplanted Edmontonian Moe Berg was scuffling around Toronto, trying desperately to get gigs. His new band recorded a four-song demo tape to shop to the clubs. Then Berg got an offer of help.

"I had this friend, Nelu Ghiran, who was a film director," Berg explains. "As a fun project, we listened to the four songs. He said, 'This is the song I think I can make a video out of.' When you think about how lucky and stupid it is to become successful, it's stuff like that. So we made the video, and all heck broke lose."

Berg dropped the video at MuchMusic, and it started getting lots of play. "I remember talking to the guy at the Rivoli and just begging him for, like, an hour, please let us play," says Berg. "So we did the show, and it was sold out. Everyone was there to see us, they'd seen the video. Then all of a sudden, calls started coming.

"It actually makes more sense as you get older."
— Eden Munro,
Vue Weekly

Instead of having to approach people, I'd get home from my job and there'd be twelve messages from agents and managers."

There was still one thing missing. "After the video came out, we'd wander into a record store and people would go, 'Where's your record?' Well, we don't have a record. And they'd go, 'People come in here every day asking to buy "I'm An Adult Now".' So, again, we didn't have a clue what we were doing. We had some friends who designed a record cover, and we got five hundred manufactured. We took them to some stores and they all went. The guy who ran the Record Peddler said, 'Why don't I take this over for you for a little bit,' and then he sold a whole bunch."

Almost a quarter-century later, "I'm An Adult Now" continues to connect with new audiences. "I guess you're always hoping as a writer that you have a relatable lyric that people can put themselves in your position or empathize with you. It struck a chord with them. The whole concept of growing up, it starts pretty early. Kids liked it because even they think they're growing up. Even when you're seventeen you think, oh my gosh, my childhood is behind me. There's probably no time in your life where you're not conscious of the fact you're getting older, your life is changing."

In 2009, Moe Berg turned fifty. Does he feel like an adult now? "I guess I have for some time now, but in some ways, I don't. That's also part of the song, this fight against it. I'm not really an adult. As much as it is about growing up, it's also about what a drag that is. How much you'd like to reconnect with the things you might have to leave behind."

33 Nothin'

The Ugly Ducklings
Yorktown, 1966

"It's punk. It's psychedelic. It's brilliant."
— Alan Wigney, *The Ottawa Sun*

By the mid-1960s, rock's biggest names were using the recording studio as a laboratory, with artists such as The Beatles and The Beach Boys spending weeks, and thousands of dollars, to perfect monumental creations such as *Sgt. Pepper's Lonely Hearts Club Band* and *Pet Sounds*. On the flip side were the garage bands. The Ugly Ducklings from Toronto managed to score a hit with much less expense.

"It was $330," remembers singer Dave Bingham. "The whole thing was financed by [guitar player] Roger Mayne. He had his first job working at the CBC, he had the money in the bank. We knew if we didn't do it, we'd end up like all the other bands in the Yorkville Village, still doing the same thing. It was one of those things where we went in and broke all the rules. We totally ignored the VU meters and just went for it. It was the sixth or eighth take — we basically recorded it live."

In just a couple of hours, the group recorded what is recognized all over the world as one of the great garage tracks of all time, a sneering, distorted piece of protopunk. It's also a classic example of no muss, no fuss, and keep it simple, stupid.

"It was the real first song we ever wrote," says Bingham, still amazed by it. "As soon as Roger played the chords for me, I knew it was special. I wrote all the lyrics, it took maybe two hours. It was recorded on my birthday in '66, June 5, the day I turned twenty. It sounds exactly like the band sounded live, no gizmos.

"I was one of those guys that was always rebelling against something. So Roger and I thought, what are we gonna write about? Because we really hadn't lived a life yet that we could write about, so I said 'Why don't we write about nothin'?' The idea of writing a song called 'Nothin' was just perfect and anti to me."

Despite lots of local love and a number one hit on several Canadian stations the next year with "Gaslight", the band broke up in 1968 and faded from the airwaves. But a decade later, obscure garage rock records were being rediscovered by a new type of audience: "All the Ducks records were really hyped during the punk years in the seventies. They had a club called the Crash 'n' Burn in Toronto in 1977. All the Ducks records were reissued, and there, the kids played them over and over. They literally wore the singles out on the jukebox, they wouldn't play any more, and that led to the Ducks' reunion in the late seventies."

Since then, "Nothin'" has been a fixture on garage rock compilations worldwide and is a must-know for any punk fan. The Ugly Ducklings' *Somewhere Outside* album has become a constant seller, a cult classic, and was voted #72 in *The Top 100 Canadian Albums*.

34 Coax Me

Sloan
Geffen, 1994

"Geffen was counting on these guys to be the next big alterna-Grunge thing, and Sloan hands them this Beatle-y, clean, catchy number. Bravo, Sloan, bravo!"

— Scott Remila, musician,
City and Colour/The Violet Archers

Already sick of the Grunge tag they'd been saddled with after their debut album, *Smeared*, Sloan had quite a change in store with their second disc, *Twice Removed*. The first single, "Coax Me", was a stylistic turnaround, with the band now revealing a sophisticated pop sound. They were a bit wordy, too: name another song with the word "cajole" in it. "There's usually one word per song to remind people that we're super-nerds," chuckles writer Chris Murphy. "The expression was one that my dad used to say to me when he was trying to wake me up to go to school: 'Don't make me coax and cajole you to get out of bed.' But the song doesn't have anything to do with that."

Many fans at the time thought the group was referring directly to the Grunge god, Kurt Cobain. "It seems to be about him," Murphy says, eager to shut down the rumour, "the idea that he dies, and the widow makes the money. But we recorded it in February 1994 and he died in April. It just came out at the time he had died, but it wasn't about him at all."

Okay, we'll bite. What is it about, Chris? "I think it's about not wanting to lose our love of the music, and the intersection you come to as a young person between doing what you love and the idea of trying to make a living and trying to negotiate those things. That's right where we were at the time."

Sloan were in the awful position of fighting with their new record label, the US powerhouse Geffen. The company brass wanted another "Underwhelmed" and a loud, Grunge-y album, which they could easily promote to the Nirvana/Pearl Jam crowd. When Sloan delivered *Twice Removed*, Geffen all but shut down the promotional efforts. That killed the album in the United States, but

Canadian fans were on board and pushed "Coax Me" into the Top Forty.

The band soldiered on, narrowly avoided a career-ending break-up, fought and won a release from Geffen, and started racking up more and more hit singles and videos home in Canada, which was just fine by them. Sloan have also managed to remain critically loved and are still considered alternative, despite closing in on twenty years together. The group have run their own indie label, but at the same time sold their songs for commercials.

It's a fine balancing act, according to Murphy: "I know that as you become more and more commercially successful, you lose your power in the cool gang and you can never go back. But we've kept one foot in the industry and one foot, hopefully, decidedly, an ironic distance from the embarrassment of just being an industry thing. I don't know where we stand at this point. Basically I'm in bed by 9:30; I don't know what's going on."

35 Closer To The Heart

Rush
Anthem, 1977

"The Canadian ambassadors of rock at their finest."
— Darin Clark, Z99

Rush had been through many ups and downs in the mid-seventies, including the disastrous "Down The Tubes Tour" of 1975, when it looked like the band were on their last legs. Luckily, the members channelled their anger and defiance against the music industry into the career-saving *2112* album, and the future looked brighter. With a hit album, FM radio support, and a growing audience, the only thing missing was a Top Forty hit, but there seemed little chance of that considering their lengthy progressive tunes.

It even seemed a remote idea to the band. Neil Peart says they never consciously tried to write a single: "No, we never did. We just got lucky a couple of times. It did surprise us."

That first surprise came from "Closer To The Heart". It was an accidental by-product of the attempts to grow after *2112*. "In the summer of 1976, we went off to rural Wales to make *A Farewell to Kings*," says Peart. "At that time we were engrossed in reinventing ourselves. After four

albums, we wanted to expand our sound beyond guitar, bass, and drums, and had even discussed adding a keyboard player. But, instead, we were adding synthesizers, acoustic guitars, and melodic percussion — all of which contribute to the musical construction of 'Closer to the Heart'."

Peart also found himself changing his writing style. This was the man who had just delivered an epic, sidelong suite about "the futuristic dystopia and the individual rediscovering music in the machine age" for *2112*. Now, he found himself drawn to a simpler theme. "A friend from the Seattle area, Peter Talbot, had showed me some of his poems," says Peart. "I liked the simple idealism of this one. He said the title came from an engraving on his grandmother's wall, with an image of a blacksmith at work — on a ploughshare, I think — and the caption was 'Mould it closer to the heart.' The first verse was Peter's alone, as I recall, and I built most of the other three to match it. The medieval imagery of

blacksmiths and ploughmen, and the somewhat 'utopian' appeal, fit well with the music, I think."

The song advises, "Philosophers and ploughmen / Each must know his part." So which is Peart? "Fact is, when I was born in 1952, we lived on the family dairy farm near Hagersville, Ontario. I still have a silver tray my father won in a ploughing match that year. Later, Dad became a farm equipment dealer in St. Catharines, and I worked for him as a kid, on holidays, and just before joining Rush, following in Dad's footsteps as a full-time parts-manager-in-training. So there's definitely a good measure of ploughman in me, but if you take the etymology of philosophy as 'lover of knowledge,' it's also true that I like to think about stuff and try to figure it out. Perhaps I am nothing more or less than a philosophizin' ploughman! That works."

36 Picture My Face

Teenage Head
IGM, 1978

"Few ever understood that The Ramones were simply Herman's Hermits in leather jackets at 78 rpm. Teenage Head did."

— Gary "Pig" Gold, writer/editor

Loud and brash and in-your-face, Hamilton's Teenage Head were one of the very first Canadian punk bands. Rather than the snotty and sloppy stance of England's punks, Teenage Head took their influences from the real roots of the music, such as the New York Dolls and classic rockabilly artists from the 1950s. For a final twist, they also had a sweet side, anticipating the future sounds of power pop.

Guitar player Gord Lewis had a deep love for the 45, and was proud as can be when "Picture My Face" came out: "That was the first thing we ever released, before any album. It was at a time when that was the thing to release, a single. With the New Wave and the punk thing from the States and England, you put out a 45. We were trying to fit into that."

Frontman Frankie Venom was one of the great characters of Canadian rock, with a captivating presence on stage. The band needed a song to match that face, and this was it. "We were making a statement, saying look at me," says Lewis. "It was kinda melancholy, kinda sad, but with that attitude."

The song structure also came from a surprising source, perhaps the least punk band ever.

"I just wanted to slow things down a bit," says Lewis. "I wanted to do something musical. The one song that influenced me a lot for it was 'A Little Bit Me, A Little Bit You' by The Monkees. It has a lot of suspended chords, and that I got from the New York Dolls. I thought it out, having an intro, verse, chorus. I wanted a melodic solo, I knew I wanted a bridge, a third section." A lot more goes into those bashed-out punk songs than people realize.

When "Picture My Face" was ready for release, Lewis and the band found out their record label wasn't going to put it out with all the dignity they thought it deserved. "They didn't want to pay for a picture sleeve — too expensive. So we went and did it, we made them ourselves. Steve designed the sleeve, and we actually went down to a printer here in Hamilton and made them up, cut them out of the cardboard, glued them together, got the raw 45s, and inserted them into the picture sleeve. So anyone who has an original copy, I can guarantee that somebody from the band glued it together."

For Gord Lewis, holding that picture sleeve and single was the moment he knew he was a songwriter and that his group was ready. "I knew we were moving on now. It was a song that cemented things for us. It connected things and helped us move on to write more. It was a catalyst. It just felt very comfortable and we were very proud of it. This is it! We can do more now, we can do an album, let's go."

Éric Trudel

When I set out to write *The Top 100 Canadian Albums*, I was concerned that francophone music would get short shrift, since this would be a book aimed at the English market. I was very relieved to find out a colleague from Quebec was working on a similar project at the same time, for the French music world. Éric Trudel is a music journalist in Montreal, contributes to various publications, and works at Musique Plus. His second book, *Les 101*

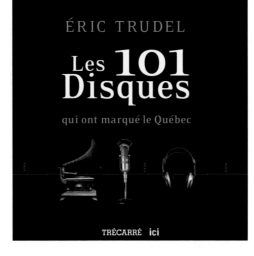

ÉRIC TRUDEL

Les **101** Disques

qui ont marqué le Québec

TRÉCARRÉ **ici**

albums qui ont marqué le Québec, detailed the best albums in history in Quebec. It was published in 2008 and received critical acclaim. I asked Éric to contribute a list of his favourite francophone singles for this book. "I decided to forgo the journalistic route," he writes, "and just go with my personal choices, off the top of my head and from the bottom of my heart. Those who know and love French music will understand; as for the others, bienvenue au Québec!"

ISADORE SOUCY

1. **DES FRAISES ET DES FRAMBOISES – Isidore Soucy**
   The original party music from Quebec. All you need is a heated room and a violin, and maybe something to drink. Isidore and his family are folk legends. One of his singles, "Prendre un verre de bière mon minou", sold 100,000 units in 1950!

2. **LE P'TIT BONHEUR – Félix Leclerc**
   Can't bypass this one. In Quebec's cultural history, there is a "before" and an "after" Félix. This man blazed the trail, and is still number one. The simpler the song . . .

3. **J'ENTENDS FRAPPER – Michel Pagliaro**
   That song was such a hit that it even reached number one on English radio stations in Kingston, Ontario. No wonder, for who can resist Pag? This man is the definitive rocker, from sea to shining sea.

4. **JE SUIS COOL – Gilles Valiquette**
   Challenged by his label to write a hit, Gilles decides to go for irony and false nonchalance, and hits the mark, all while staying cool. Success is so easy . . . isn't it? Get your money for nothing and your chicks for free.

FÉLIX LECLERC

MICHEL PAGLIARO

5. **CE SOIR ON DANSE NAZILAND –
Nanette Workman**

An Amazon sings about dancing off the apocalypse in a penthouse dance club, backed by a fantastic disco track laden with strings. Taken from the rock opera *Starmania*, one of the greatest French albums, courtesy of Michel Berger and Luc Plamondon.

6. **CASH MOE – Corbeau**

Two minutes and thirty-eight seconds of raw, unadulterated, and raunchy rock and roll. Great opening salvo from a super tight outfit, fronted by a dynamo called Marjo.

7. **ALYS EN CINÉMASCOPE – Diane Dufresne**

One of our greatest stars pays a stirring tribute to a predecessor, Alys Robi, who sang around the world in the forties. It's about show business cycles and ephemeral success . . . makes me want to cry every time I hear it.

8. **ON VEUT PAS PAYER – Madame**

The economic crisis and the failed Referendum created a drought in French music in the first half of the eighties. Great time for reinvention, and this UFO from a six-piece band of artists from Jonquière is a fine example.

9. **ISABELLE – Jean Leloup**

Irresistible, genius, crazy, Leloup's all that on his good days, and the day he created this jumping song was one of his best! And the video — a pastiche of Jean-Luc Godard's 1960 nouvelle vague movie, *À bout de souffle* — by Jean's buddy James di Salvio is also a gem.

10. **ÉTOILES FILANTES – Les Cowboys Fringants**

This song is already a classic. Years from now, it'll still be played and sung, and it'll still move whoever listens. Why? Because it reminds us that we are like shooting stars: we will come to pass, but in the meantime, we can shine.

11. **COMPTER LES CORPS – Vulgaires Machins** Our brightest talents aren't necessarily our biggest stars. This outfit continue to thrive under the radar by doling out spiky social commentaries and muscular music. Great punk rock, with brains! This one's a tank: YouTube it, and thank me when you meet me.

37 Shakin' All Over

The Guess Who
Quality, 1965

"Their rendition stands as a garage rock classic."
— Lou Molinaro, promoter

Back in the early 1960s, when Winnipeg's Randy Bachman was learning guitar, he was wild for all things British, from The Beatles to The Shadows with ace guitarist Hank Marvin. For his band Chad Allan and The Reflections, he developed a pipeline to England. "We were not writing our own songs yet," Bachman says of that band. "Well, we were, but they were terrible, so we were looking for previous hits to cover. We got sent a reel-to-reel tape from a British cousin of a friend of the band. We heard 'Shakin' All Over' [by Johnny Kidd and The Pirates] and decided to record it, plus some other songs on the tape. They were proven hits in the UK, and we thought maybe they would catch on in North America."

This wasn't Abbey Road in London. This was Winnipeg. "The whole band plugged into [bassist] Jim Kale's Fender concert amp," Bachman remembers. "We had a microphone in the middle of a cement room in the CJAY television station. We set up the gear around that mike. Chad Allen sang into it, and it picked the rest of us up from the sound of the room. We balanced our two guitars, the bass, and the piano in the concert amp, which had four inputs. When we heard about the fifth playback, where the engineer forgot to unplug a cord from the patch bay and mistakenly created an Elvis-type slapback echo, we all said, 'That's the take.' It has mistakes and goofs in it, but it is a great performance and a magical moment captured on tape."

What happens next is a bit murky. Legend has it the record company wanted to fool disc jockeys into thinking this was some hot new British group, maybe even The Beatles, and sent out a few copies with the words "Guess Who?" on them. Bachman has a different version of events: "Chad Allen and The Reflections had to change the name of the band because of a hit record called 'Just Like Romeo & Juliet' by The Reflections. So we were nameless. George Struth at Quality Records kept asking, 'What's the band name? I want to release the record,' and we couldn't come up with a name fast enough. So he released a white label 45 that said in big black letters: 'SHAKIN' ALL OVER — GUESS WHO?' The record went to number one in Canada and got released in the States on Scepter Records and went to number twenty-two on the Billboard charts. Like it or not, we were called 'Guess Who.' Sometimes, we put THE in front of it."

Believing the US market was now open to them, the renamed band headed for New York. Tough tours and a flop follow-up single sent them back to Winnipeg. Chad Allan and keyboard player Bob Ashley quit. The next time the group hit the charts, they would have a new lead singer and be ready with great material of their own.

38 Signs

Five Man Electrical Band
Lionel, 1971

First, there was a song. Not "Signs" — that came later. The song that started things was "Five Man Electrical Band", by the Ottawa group The Staccatos. "It was a strange thing, we were voted the number one band in Canada as The Staccatos," says lead singer Les Emmerson. "Then we go and change our name. Not a great business move. Before, we were a cover band. But we decided that if the band was going to do anything, we were going to have to stand and fall on our own stuff. So we changed our name and our style. We took a monetary beating for a while."

The band changed their name in 1969, and Emmerson started working on "Signs", an us-versus-them story set in the generation gap. "There was a friend of mine and his girlfriend, both were refused jobs even though they were quite capable, just because of the way they looked. I got mad at that, thinking that shouldn't have anything to do with it. It wasn't as if they were dealing with the public. They were very smart people.

"The line 'you gotta have a membership card to get inside' came from this bar we were playing. It was a golf and country club. What you did was you paid a dollar or two at the door and you became a member for the night. That was the loophole of how people were let in."

The Staccatos had been so successful in Canada that the new group signed a US contract and started recording in Los Angeles. "Signs", however, was not the focus. "Mike Curb, the head of MGM, he loved the other side," says Emmerson of the song "Hello Melinda Goodbye". "He dropped into the studio the night we were recording it and really liked it. So he wanted that. And our producer, Dallas Smith, went nuts. He was begging them. He said, 'No, you're on the wrong side of this record, please!'

"We came back to Canada because we had run out of money. We were in Burlington at the Tree Top Lounge and got a call from our producer. He says, 'Listen guys, I want to switch labels.' And we went, are you nuts? We went to so much trouble to get this. And he says, 'I don't care, there's this little label in New York called Lionel Records. The guy's very keen, he wants to go with "Signs".' If it wasn't for Dallas Smith, we would never have had this hit. He pushed and pushed, he said, 'I can smell it, taste it, it's a hit record.' So we changed to Lionel Records and it went through the roof. Then, after it was riding the top of the charts, MGM came over and bought Lionel Records, so we're back under that umbrella again. This business is just bizarre."

> "Les Emmerson's voice had such angst and passion."
>
> — Lou Molinaro, promoter

39 Lost Together

Blue Rodeo
Warner, 1992

"Can a ballad be anthemic? Blue Rodeo proves that it can with this lovely heartbreaker."

— Michael Elves, writer, UMFM

A lot of what makes Blue Rodeo such a strong and long-lasting band is the unique partnership of Jim Cuddy and Greg Keelor. From the start of the group's fame, with the hit "Try", the duo's roles became well established. Cuddy was the sensitive singer of ballads, Keelor the wild card, with guitar rockers. It is a bit more complicated.

Jim Cuddy knows there's a bigger picture of his partner: "Greg and I have always been characterized as one being the cynic and one being the opposite. We are, of course, not that contrasted. Greg is a very sentimental and heartfelt guy, he just expresses it differently."

Every once and a while, Keelor reminds listeners of his other side. "Lost Together" was perhaps the first. "I think that was a great moment for Greg," says Cuddy. "'Lost Together' was remarkable. I remember Greg singing it on a bus when we were travelling. And I remember making fun of him a little bit because, at that point, Greg did not write sentimentally.

He would write with a sense of melancholy, but not sentimental. That was quite a sentimental notion, that if we're lost, we're lost together. I think I callously made fun of him, that he was getting soft. He took, as he should, great offence to that. I think it was a watershed moment for Greg's writing. It opened him up to allow himself to be a little bit more emotionally vulnerable in songs."

Cuddy acknowledges this close partnership with Keelor is the key to the band. Both have ventured out with solo careers, but there has never been a hint of a permanent break, or even a vacation. Tours and albums come like clockwork. Here's how Cuddy explains their relationship: "I think Greg and I share a lot of sensibilities. We certainly share what we think is good music and how we think we should operate and act as a band. And we really share a sense of humour. Those things are very bridging for us because we are very different people. We are as we appear, in terms of our outlook on life. He is

more cynical and I am more upbeat. So, in a way, those stereotypes are true, but they just don't tell the whole truth. I don't think Greg and I have ever sweated about being pigeonholed as being one thing or another. Greg is comfortable with the way people see him, and I'm certainly comfortable with the way people see me.

"I think we have been able to co-exist as partners because we are different. If I'm not around Greg for a while, I miss his take on life. I miss also being able to share my take on life with him, because I know he will never take offence. It's a good partnership in that regard. So we've been lucky to have somebody that close to share this life with."

40 Sonny's Dream

Ron Hynes
Grand East, 1981

There really was a Sonny. He is Ron Hynes's uncle, Thomas O'Neill, and he means a great deal to his nephew. "We're talking about the man who taught me how to play guitar," Hynes says. "Taught me accordion, gave me my first love of song, Sonny. When I started going to my grandmother's place as a kid, he was a great lover of song, he was a big fan of Johnny Cash, he was a huge Marty Robbins fan. He was a really, really big influence on me, because he was always and forever singing these songs. So by the time I was ten or eleven years old, I knew what I wanted to be in my life. I knew I wanted to be a songwriter."

Sonny's story is about living in a remote area and wondering if life could be better elsewhere, and if he should go. "He lived up in Long Beach," Hynes says of Sonny, "which is just this side of Cape Race, the most northeasterly point in North America, if you discount Cape Spear. That whole community, I don't think ever in its existence it had more than forty or fifty people in that small community.

And when everybody had moved out, moved on, relocated to larger centres, my grandmother and Sonny were the last people who were there. He was that little boy, he lived on a farm on a wide-open space, which is to say it's a Newfoundland farm, where there's fishing and farming involved. He was the boy who walked to the highway and imagined what it was like to be somewhere else, to be in St. John's, to be a hundred miles to town."

"Sonny's Dream" is a folksong, and got treated as such. Irish musicians visiting Canada heard it, and it was passed on by what's called the "folk process." In other words, they borrowed it, rewrote it, passed it on, and that version got rewritten. "Sonny's Dream" was such a hit in Ireland that most people there assume it's a traditional song. The folk process

continued, as American artists such as Chet Atkins and Emmylou Harris heard their Irish friends' versions and brought it back across the ocean.

Ron Hynes owes a lot to his Uncle Sonny — his career and his biggest hit. "I knew emphatically this was what I wanted to do, and that all comes from him," says Hynes. "It's amazing that that song became the most known song of my career, my most famous work. And I guess it's rightfully so, because

> "When Ron explained how he wrote it, the crowded nightclub was so quiet you could hear a pin drop."
>
> — Ron Gillespie, Ocean 100

he was the one who instilled that love of song in me."

There's only one problem with the whole story, of Sonny's life and Ron's career: Sonny doesn't think it's true. "If anybody says that to him, he'll say, 'That song is not about me, that song is about Ron. Ron is writing about himself and his father.'" Maybe Sonny's dream was Ron's dream all along.

SIRE®

STATIK

SIDE ONE

25 99567
Q
(99567-A)

Time: 2:44
Pub: Tactik
Music

From the
Statik Album
"RHYTHM
OF
YOUTH"
STAT 10

THE SAFETY DANCE
(Ivan)
MEN WITHOUT HATS
Produced by Marc Durand
℗ 1982 Statik Records

SIRE RECORDS INC. MANUFACTURED AND DISTRIBUTED BY/FABRIQUE ET DISTRIBUE PAR · WEA MUSIC OF CANADA, LTD. 1810 BIRCHMOUNT RD. SCARBOROUGH, ONT. / WARNER COMMUNICATIONS COMPANY

41 The Safety Dance

Men Without Hats

Statik, 1982

"Canada's 'YMCA'."

— Rebecca Case, manager

You can dance if you want to. It was a call to the dance floor for music fans standing on the sidelines through the whole disco era. Ivan Doroschuk, the leader of the Montreal band, was a fan of new music and he wanted to dance to those sounds. "It came out of a direct experience," he says. "It was in Ottawa. We would go to clubs, and the New Wave and punk music — they weren't playing much of it; it was still pretty much disco and heavy rock. Every time they'd play a punk or New Wave song, we'd start dancing and pogoing. We'd usually get kicked off the dance floor and thrown out of the club by the bouncers, or told by the management to tone it down. So I went home and I wanted to tell people, don't let these bouncers say we can't dance to New Wave if we want to."

It was the dancers who made it a hit. "I don't even think the single charted Top Ten in Canada, the first time around," Doroschuk remembers. "We were in the studio doing the second record when the dance mix hit number one on the dance chart. Then the Americans started lining up outside our door to throw contracts at us. We signed, and the thing started shooting up the charts. It was on tour when we did the video and people started recognizing me on the street."

Oh yes, that video. Men Without Hats created one of the iconic films of the medium, still a visual and quirky treat. It had brilliant colours, real British morris dancers, and a dwarf. Plus, Ivan looked like no one else in 1982. "People were surprised by my long hair, they weren't expecting that and they weren't expecting that medieval video either. People didn't have long hair then, and if they did, it was gelled straight up."

The video itself was an expensive risk, according to Doroschuk: "It was the early days, when people weren't sure if this video thing was going to fly. It was shot in Bath, England. They actually flew me over on Concorde. I only had three days of a window to shoot it."

Then Doroschuk headed straight back to the road. "It started snow-balling, and things were just getting bigger and bigger. We were on ground zero as it was happening. We went from travelling from a van, we moved up to a Winnebago, and then a tour bus, and then two tour buses. We went from sleeping on people's coaches to motels to hotels to good hotels to great hotels."

The song leaped from the dance charts and the New Wave audience to conquer the video and Top Forty channels. "What people liked was the message. It was a rallying cry: you can dance if you want to. You didn't have to be a New Wave fan. People just liked the message of being empowered."

42 Claire

Rheostatics
Sire, 1994

"My future wife told me she was head over heels for me while we were sitting cross-legged right in front of the stage watching the Rheostatics. Our daughter's middle name is Claire."

— Ken Beattie, publicity

Rheostatics' lone entry onto the pop charts came about completely backwards. Beloved by a cult audience of critics, college students, and musicians, The group had no intention of bothering the Top Forty. It happened because of a soundtrack hit, from a movie based on a successful book. Instead of the usual chronology, the band named an album after the book first, way before there was a movie or a soundtrack.

1992's *Whale Music* had nothing to do with author Paul Quarrington's book of the same name, but Rheostatics were looking to make a statement. "Canadian music at the time was sort of sneered at," says founding member Dave Bidini. "So we thought naming our album after a governor general's award-winning book was our attempt to have music considered on par with all the other Canadian art forms."

The band met with Quarrington to ask permission to use his title. A few months later, *Whale Music* was about to become a film, and the group were offered the soundtrack. "It was our job to crawl into the head of the main character, Desmond," Bidini says. "It wasn't hard for a group to do that — he was a musician holed up in his mansion. This is his love song, his ode to Claire. When we were planning the songwriting roles, [Rheostatic] Tim Vesely had already composed the song. He had jumped the gun, the bastard! In a band with three writers, you have to be quick. We played it for the producers and Paul Quarrington, and they were amazed we were able to write a basic verse-chorus-verse pop song. We had aspired to do that before, but never could. I don't think we could have without being assigned it. We were pretending to be a pop group and it worked."

Having a hit single was completely foreign to the group, Bidini admits. "That whole concept was a distraction. We were an albums band. We always cared about album sequences, mood, and theme. I remember being at my doctor and hearing it on the radio, with the announcer talking about it. It was amusing. I don't think we took it that seriously, we didn't want to be rated by our chart success. Maybe we should have, though, because it did open up a new audience for us. We've met dozens of people since who have named their daughter or their pet after it. It made new connections. But we knew that, of our three-and-a-half-minute radio reserve of songs, that was it."

It was not, however, the end of the connection with Paul Quarrington: "We all got to be very good friends. He became a mentor on the writing side, a hero to me, with his books *Whale Music*, *King Leary*, and *Home Game*. Super important to me as friend." Bidini is now a celebrated author of sports and cultural books, including *The Best Game You Can Name* and *On A Cold Road: Tales of Adventure in Canadian Rock*.

43 One Fine Morning
Lighthouse
GRT, 1970

"A better sound than Chicago but no fame for Canadians!"
— Philip Carr, music fan

Drummers aren't normally the leaders of rock bands, but Skip Prokop had all the skills needed. He'd been a songwriter at sixteen and had led the successful Toronto band The Paupers. After that, he became a go-to drummer and bandleader, working with Janis Joplin, Carlos Santana, and Al Kooper. His most important gig, though, was with Mama Cass.

"One of the things that really bothered me," says Prokop, "was that you would hear bands on the radio and say, wow, I really like that song. Then you'd go to see them, and they didn't sound like they did on record. I started thinking about it. With Cass Elliot, we were the first rock band to go into Vegas. We had a seven-piece band, and where I was sitting on the riser, my back was to a fifty-six-piece orchestra. It was unbelievable. There's such power in a big sound like that. I thought it would be amazing if you put a band together that had a rock nucleus, it would have brass, and an electric string quartet,

which would allow you to do anything you wanted in the studio and reproduce it on stage."

That was Lighthouse. "We were doing major gigs without any kind of hit record," Prokop relates. "The word went out all over the place — you gotta see this band, man. As far as a rock ensemble [was concerned], nobody had ever seen anything like this massive, thirteen-piece band. We were the first rock band invited to the Newport Jazz Festival, the first at the Monterey Jazz Festival."

Still, they weren't selling many records. "Our manager said, 'This producer, Jimmy Ienner, thinks you're a great writer, and he believes if he could spend some time with you, you could get hit records.' We got together, just studying: why is this a hit? What he did for me was open up a whole bunch of doors in my head."

"One Fine Morning" happened in London, England. "I had gone for a walk down some of the old-town

streets, the little shops. That was the thing that blew me away. In Canada, you look at a building that says 1838 and you go, wow, is that ever old. When you're in England, you look at buildings that say 603. I went into the hotel, sat on the bed, picked up my guitar, and just wrote the song. It was bam-boom-done, that fast."

The other important element was new lead singer Bob McBride. "One Fine Morning" put Lighthouse in the Top Ten, and *Lighthouse Live* became the first Canadian album to go platinum in the United States. "It was totally different when we went back to Carnegie Hall. The first four bars, we hit that and the place was on their feet, the whole place erupted. We hadn't sung a word. And I remember looking at Ralph [Cole, guitar] and thinking, you knew you had made it when that happened."

44 (Make Me Do) Anything You Want

A Foot In Coldwater
Daffodil, 1972

"One of the first bands I can remember going, cool, they are Canadian."
— Andy Curran, SRO Management

Drummer and songwriter Danny Taylor had already seen two great chances to make it in the music world fall apart. Taylor and Foot bassist Hughie Leggat had been in the mid-sixties Toronto bubblegum band Lords of London, who'd scored a number one hit in Toronto in 1967 with "Cornflakes And Ice Cream". "I was still in junior high," says Taylor. "We had that big hit and we were about fifteen years old. It was taking us to places my parents had never been, flying to New York and Cleveland and doing these TV shows. It was a dream come true."

The dream was over just as fast. Arguments over the follow-up single that was supposed to break them in the States caused them to break up. Most of them regrouped as Nucleus. Much loved in Toronto's Yorkville scene, they landed a record deal and US tour. But once again, internal band problems hit, and they broke up. "It took us a long time to get there, and unfortunately we couldn't realize the dream," says Taylor, still disappointed today.

He wasn't going to give up on the group, though. The nucleus of Nucleus, Taylor, Leggat, and keyboard player Bob Horne, welcomed new members Paul Naumann on guitar and singer Alex Machin. "Paul and I were experimenting with different tunings," remembers Taylor. "We were tuning the Es down to Ds, trying to create some magic." Taylor had reached what he describes as a crisis: "I had been in two bands and both of them had promise of success, one with a number one record, the other with a tour. Both bands broke up, and I was extremely distraught over the whole thing. But I thought this was a good band. I think it was soul searching. I was looking for some inspiration and some reason to even be here."

He reached out to a higher power. "I was actually on my knees, saying, Why have you brought me here? Why have you taken me to this point? You took me away from home, you put me through all these trials and tribulations. For what? What do you want from me? What am I supposed to do? And Paul had been playing these chords, and I just listened to it, and I said, 'Whatever it is you want me to do, make me do it, help me to do it.' And when I said these words, and Paul was playing this thing, he said, 'Woah! What did you just say?' and I said, 'Make me do anything you want!' And he looks at me and goes, 'Oh!' And a big smile came on his face.

"Everybody thinks it's a love song. I know it's played at a lot of weddings, I know a lot of girlfriends sing it to their boyfriends." But that interpretation doesn't bother him. "I heard one disc jockey say it was probably the most romantic song she ever heard. I had to swallow hard."

45 Sunglasses At Night

Corey Hart
Aquarius, 1983

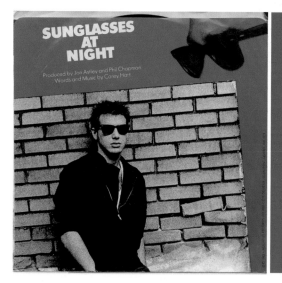

"It helped put Canada on the map
as a purveyor of current music."

— Jenna Chow, CBC Radio

Here's the story in Corey Hart's own words: "In the early spring of '83, I was a starry-eyed nineteen-year-old kid from Montreal recording in a studio near Manchester, England. By late May, approaching my twentieth birthday, I finally held in my hands a cassette which contained the finished recordings of eleven original songs that would comprise my *First Offense* album debut.

"However, there was one more song to come. Track twelve, 'Sunglasses At Night'. It was not yet written, but the idea had already begun a subterranean journey through my creative subconscious. It rained almost every day I was in the UK for those sessions. I had a pair of Ray Ban sunglasses with me but I never had the chance to use them.

"Later that summer, my album was delivered to Aquarius-Capitol Records. Everyone seemed very pleased with the results. I was kinda like a writing magnet in those days, so the song ideas kept flowing even though we were

done with the recording. I started messing around with a melodic line and phrase called 'My Cigarette Got Wet'. It is an ironic lyric because I have never smoked in my life.

"One night I went back to the 'Wet' demo and sang out the lines 'I Wear My Sunglasses At Night' over the melody. Wow. Just like that the song was born. It now spirited a cooler cadence from the new lyric that was missing before, plus I changed a few chord progressions. I wanted to add it to my album on the spot. Impossible, I thought; we'd already spent the full recording budget. But I will call the label first thing in the morning anyway and plead my case.

"To their credit and intuition, Aquarius Records sent me back to England. They trusted me when I told them, 'I think this one is really good.' My producers in London, Phil Chapman and Jon Astley, brought out the best in the song. They brilliantly produced the track highlighting the hip sounds and styles exploding out of

the UK music scene during that prolific period in the early eighties.

"When it was released in November 1983, I remember hearing the song for the first time on CHOM-FM in Montreal, but I only caught thirty seconds before I blew out my car speakers because I had cranked the volume up to overload!

"Last week I was on a crowded rental shuttle bus at Miami Airport on my way to pick up our car. The radio was blaring out 'China Girl' by David Bowie. As the tune faded out, it segued into the next song. I heard the hypnotic intro riff of 'Sunglasses At Night' fill the air. Some folks started to tap their feet. I glanced over at my thirteen-year-old daughter. We both had big smiles on our faces. Yeah man, it still feels super cool to hear it — even after all these years."

LOVERBOY

Get Lucky

46 Working For The Weekend

Loverboy
CBS, 1981

The kids at the Little River Band concert in Vancouver didn't know they were witnessing the birth of one of the country's rock anthems. "I was the CFOX fox, dressed up in a fox outfit," laughs Paul Dean. This was when he and Mike Reno were just starting up what became Loverboy. "Mike was my roadie. We didn't have nothing, we didn't have a band, but the two of us were writing and working together. And here was an opportunity to make

> "The Friday night mullet anthem, the song never fails to bring out the air guitar."
>
> — Evan Newman, manager

two hundred dollars between the two of us. I would go up and just riff on my guitar and amp between bands, promoting the station. We opened, I guess you could say, for Little River Band. I took off my outfit, and sat in the audience, and marvelled at the bass sound, how incredibly tight and clean it was. I went up on stage after, checked out the guy's rig, and found out what he was doing."

That was the bass sound Paul Dean wanted a couple of years later when he was co-producing Loverboy's second album, *Get Lucky*. He'd been working on a song that he and Reno were sure would be a hit. "I got the germ of the lyrics walking around Vancouver. It was a sunny day, a lazy day, and it struck me that nobody's doing anything, they're waiting for the weekend to let loose. I was calling it 'Waiting For The Weekend', and Mike said, How about 'Working For The Weekend?' Ya, that works, it's a cool twist on it.

"I think I said, 'You wanna piece of my heart?' and Mike says, 'You better start from the start.'" So Dean changed the title again. "I took the album down to Columbia in New York. The first song was 'You Want A Piece Of My Heart'. Paul Atkinson, our A&R director, used to be in The Zombies.

He was a real cool guy. I had a lot of respect for him; we listened to what he said. He said, 'You should call it "Working For The Weekend", man.' And I went, Okay, it didn't make any difference to me. In hindsight, it's a pretty cool title."

Road tests were going well, too. "We were playing a pub in Nanaimo, just a typical meat market on a Friday night. We finished the first two sets and the dance floor was completely empty. We opened the third set with 'Working For The Weekend' and the dance floor was packed. It was the first time we'd ever played it live. That's why it was first on the album — we knew it was going to be the first single, even before we recorded it we knew that was the one."

It remains Loverboy's most popular song, even though times have changed: "Along with everybody else during these tough economic times, we're *all* working on the weekend. That's a Mike Reno line, I have to give him the quote on it."

47 Raise A Little Hell

Trooper
MCA, 1978

"You'd have to go a long way to find a Canadian who doesn't know this weekend party anthem."

— Chris Harding, BX 93

The recording of Trooper's best-loved single is another example of a lucky accident. Several of the songs in this book revolve around such accidents and mistakes, and Randy Bachman's name keeps popping up. "American Woman" happened after he broke a string, and "You Ain't Seen Nothin' Yet" featured his stuttered vocals, meant only as a joke. For "Raise A Little Hell", Bachman was the producer who asked for one more.

Trooper leader Ra McGuire recalls how the undervalued song ended up on tape. "Back in the days of ten-song albums, we found ourselves nearing the end of the *Thick As Thieves* sessions with only nine. Randy asked if we had any more, and we pulled out the song we'd been closing our set with for years. We were so used to having it around, we'd forgotten all about it. It's funny — we played the song to close the set because people loved it, but we made three albums before it occurred to us to record it!"

It had actually been around longer than that. "I clearly remember being pissed off about something and singing the 'raise a little hell' phrase over and over. I was on the back porch of my parents' house in Fraserview [near Vancouver] — I was probably sixteen."

Maybe it's the pissed-off sixteen-year-old in all of us that made "Raise A Little Hell" part of Canadian culture. McGuire can't put his finger on the point where a song crosses over to iconic status, but he does know some of the recipe: "I think a song needs to sound real in some way. A lyric needs to feel like you're hearing someone's thoughts. The music needs to feel like the lyric. I know lots of people do have formulas, but if you take a quick look across our catalogue, you can see that we jump all over the place stylistically. 'Hell' is a whole different animal than 'We're Here For A Good Time.'"

McGuire takes no credit for the enduring success the song has had in Canada. "As with all of our songs, the magic happens with the folks who embrace them as their own. So, it's — sadly — a process we're left out of. 'Raise A Little Hell' has gone on to have a life of its own that really has nothing to do with us in many ways. Heard it yesterday at the Stanley Cup game!

"People seem to absorb their favourite songs. They take them into themselves and make them part of the fabric of their lives. I do that. Folks hardly ever discuss the songs with me in terms of the melody or the lyric. They're far more likely to tell me the song is 'their' song and then describe the ways in which it has been part of their life. It was played at their grad or their wedding or their best friend's funeral. It can be a pretty emotional connection and I never take it lightly."

48 Rise Up

Parachute Club
Current/RCA, 1983

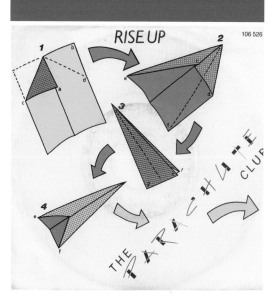

Most bands are formed for basic reasons. In the words of Bryan Adams and Jim Vallance, kids wanna rock. A few bands have a concept. Toronto's Parachute Club had even more — a vision. Lorraine Segato is the group's lead singer: "We were (a) political; (b) danceable; and (c) celebratory. We were trying to break new ground in whatever we could, politics and music. We were four women, three men, and we wanted to show that women could be players, in music and the world. And we wanted to show that politics could be danceable, too. We wanted to have a signature voice."

Parachute Club were fixtures on the Queen Street West scene, which in the early eighties was the place to be for music, arts, and social movements in Toronto. Many people in that scene felt they were part of a revolution. "We came out of a time when the idea of censorship was a very big discussion here," says Segato. "Art projects were being censored. It wasn't the kind of diverse society that you see now.

The people were there, but they were struggling to be heard. Toronto was so conservative and blueblood. Where we came from on Queen, there was a discourse on what art was, and what race was, and immigration — there was a movement of substance. This was 1983, the Cold War, Reagan, there was a recession. We envisioned a world where tolerance would be accepted. If we collectively rise and share our powers, we are so much stronger."

So it was a band with a vision. Now it needed an anthem. "It started with a groove, because we had been to Trinidad to study music. There was a melody but we didn't have a lot of lyrics for it. My best friend, filmmaker and poet Lynne Fernie, said, 'I have these words that are sort of a spirit thing.' Daniel Lanois, the producer, helped us piece it together, the big chorus, the signature groove, he really loved it."

"Rise Up" was the perfect song for everyone who wanted to stand up and be counted. Its message of inclusion meant any group on Queen Street, in Canada, or beyond could use it to connect. "A lot of people claim it as their own," Segato confirms. "The gay movement, the women's movement, every group. We went to England, and they were playing it on Christian radio as a gospel song. I feel a tremendous amount of gratitude. I should do a 'Rise Up' book, because everybody comes up and tells me what the song

> "Pure pop with a proud political agenda."
>
> — John Threlfall,
> music writer

means to them. Tremendous stories, about autism for instance.

"There was a period of time when I completely forgot about the song, but it keeps coming back in waves. The Obama thing started it again. Little waves that come up, and every time, I'm completely shocked. It was just a call to equality."

49 Black Velvet

Alannah Myles
Atlantic, 1989

"It's Alannah's gritty emotional vocal performance, and that catchy bass over the loping low-tempo groove that gets me, plus it's about the King!"

— Geoff Kulawick, True North Records

Ontario singer Alannah Myles, after years of hard work, had had a strong career. It just wasn't in the right field. "I had become a successful commercial actress in Canada," she says, "with TV spots airing on both Canadian and US stations, small roles in film and TV, various runway and print modelling jobs, taught makeup classes . . . and was a managing hostess for a chic night club. I would work on songs I had written, like 'Lover Of Mine' for my CD, with 'Funkytown' and 'I Will Survive' pumping out of disco speakers until closing time. I earned a substantial income from my commercial acting and modelling but spent every cent on my music demos to try and get a record deal, which was continually denied me as it was thought that women had babies, not careers."

Finally, her demos caught the right ears, and Myles got started on her self-titled debut. While she was writing her own material, her partner, songwriter Christopher Ward, had his own pet project, about Elvis. "Christopher penned the song while on a junket with a busload of Elvis fans touring the Graceland Mansion in Memphis, just after I had been signed to Atlantic Records. He returned from the trip having produced a TV special for MuchMusic with an acoustic version of 'Black Velvet'. From the first line of the song, I was riveted in my seat and instantly worried of who might lay their grubby mitts on it to prevent my recording it first. It was tailored for my voice, sultry, dark, and foreboding. I instantly loved it. I still do."

Myles got the track for herself, but it almost got buried in the overall sound of the rest of her debut. "It was one of the last songs written to fill out a ten-song, predominantly rock record, and though we each found ourselves mesmerized by the final recording of it, it was not until Christopher came to me on bended knee, while mixing the track at Atlantic Studios in New York City, and pleaded for me to help him convince [producer] David Tyson to throw out all the rock guitars and reduce it to mainly a bass beat and acoustic guitar, identifying its shuffle groove so that my vocal would dominate the track. It was probably the best decision I have ever made in the mixing stages of recording, quite possibly changing the course of music history."

That's not a bold claim. "Black Velvet" was number one in much of the world, and won Myles a Grammy Award, Junos, plus she sold an unprecedented million copies of her debut disc in Canada and six million worldwide. With all these accolades and milestones, Myles has a different, favourite memento. "My fondest memory was being informed by the folks who ran the Elvis fan club that Elvis's daughter Lisa Marie would love to have recorded it. I felt as though we had done her proud."

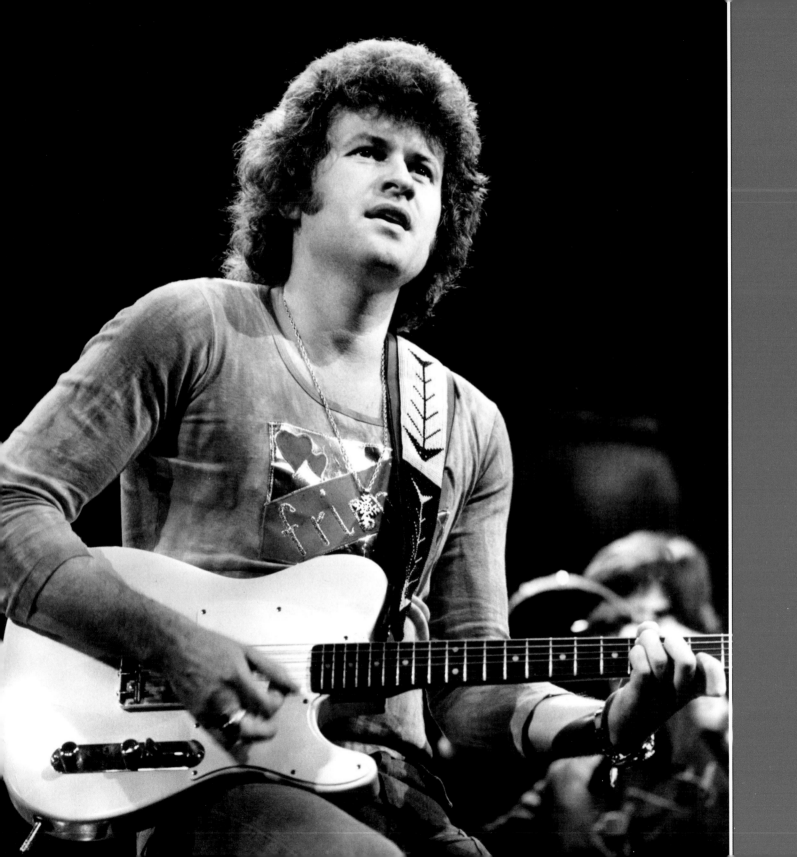

50 Seasons In The Sun

Terry Jacks
Goldfish, 1974

It was the biggest hit The Beach Boys never had. The group was stymied by the inactivity of their leader, Brian Wilson, then at the peak of his mental illness. They were looking for outside producers and songs. "Carl Wilson and Al Jardine both asked if I would produce them. We'd been friends," says Terry Jacks, writer and producer of The Poppy Family hits. "They knew I liked The Beach Boys, and Brian was out of it then."

Jacks needed a song for the group, and it came from a sad encounter. "I had a friend I was out golfing with, and he told me he had six months to live. I had a number one song in Canada with 'Concrete Sea', I was doing some touring, and when I came back, he had passed away. I remembered this song, 'Le moribond' by Jacques Brel, he was saying goodbye to everything. It had been translated from French to English by Rod McKuen. It was sort of a tongue-in-cheek song, an old man saying goodbye. But when my friend died, I wondered what it would have

been like for him to tell people he was dying, I rewrote the lyrics to match that. I recorded it, and all my friends said, 'This sucks, Jacks.' They knew my friend, they thought it was too much. It sat around for a while, I didn't know what to do with it."

He offered it up to The Beach Boys, but discovered he was in the middle of the group's infamous family wars. "None of The Beach Boys were hanging together, you had to bring them in separately. It wasn't unified because Brian had gone crazy. It was an honour to produce them, but I couldn't get the group together. I was just turning into a nervous wreck. I said, 'I can't do this anymore.' I just left. The thing never got done."

Jacks went back to his own version. This time, instead of his friends, he

played it for a younger audience. "My paperboy was there, he was listening to some of the songs. He said, 'Holy cow, this is some song.' He didn't know my friend who had died. The next day, he came by with about eight friends, and they loved it. That's why it says on the

> "I love the seventies music and have many fond memories listening to my AM radio and hearing this one."
>
> — Anna Zee, Q104

album, 'To the kids from Copper Cove.'"

Not everybody loved it. Despite selling millions of copies worldwide, it seems to have as many detractors. "Lots of disc jockeys hated it," says Jacks, still amused by the battle. "I got a call from a deejay at WABC New York, and he said on the air, 'I hate this record.' But he said he'd have a contest — if more people hated it, he'd drop it off the Empire State Building. Of course, he lost, and had to drive around the city with things stuck on his car saying he loved it."

Stuart McLean

When I asked Stuart, the host of CBC Radio's *The Vinyl Cafe*, to compose a list of his Top 10 Canadian hits, little did I know he'd take the assignment so seriously. In the end, he turned it into a full episode of his radio show, which aired in February 2010. Stuart switched the rules a little bit, and instead decided to make it a history of his connection to, and love affair with, Canadian music, growing up in Montreal. So here it is, a sort of musical autobiography of Montreal-born Stuart McLean, featuring some of the comments he made on his radio program.

1. **THEME FROM "A SUMMER PLACE" – Percy Faith and His Orchestra**
This is more or less what pop music sounded like when I became aware of pop music. This was a huge hit. It is still, I read on the web, the longest-running number one instrumental in the history of the Billboard Hot 100 singles chart. Percy Faith, who was a Toronto-raised violinist, turned to arranging and conducting when his hands were burned in a fire. He was so good at it that his lush string-soaked arrangements laid the ground for a whole genre of music. Percy Faith of Toronto is the Godfather of Easy Listening, or that's what I read. I read that on the web, too.

2. **SH-BOOM – The Crew Cuts**
Four boys from Toronto's St. Mike's Choir School who worked under a variety of names until a Cleveland disc jockey dubbed them The Crew Cuts. Rather than being people with long hair, the longhairs were into classical music in those days. This is where music started for me, with boy groups like these guys.

3. **LITTLE DARLIN' – The Diamonds**
I got this song as a premium gift from Steve's Radio Repair Shop on Westminster Avenue. in 1958. They had a promotion where you could earn a free record for every three you bought. The Diamonds were a Toronto quartet who covered songs by the black musicians who couldn't get airplay in the fifties. "Little Darlin'" was originally recorded by The Gladiolas. I didn't have a choice of what free record I got and I didn't particularly like this song when I got it. I include it because it was the first rock record I ever owned, and I was wrong about it, too. It is a great song.

4. **TALK TO ME OF MENDOCINO – Kate and Anna McGarrigle**
There was a time when every university had a couple of thriving coffee houses within an easy stone's throw, and jean-clad folksingers with their guitar cases and harmonica holders thumbed their way from one joint to the next. In Montreal, we had the Back Door, and the Yellow Door, and the Potpourri, and, on Victoria Avenue., Shimon Ash's Finjan Club. There were more. Jack Nissenson, along with Kate and Anna McGarrigle, was a member of the Mountain City Four. Chris Rawlings, Bruce Murdoch, The Mountain City Four, Michael Nuremberg, and Jesse Winchester were some of the prominent Montreal folksinging regulars. There was hardly ever more than about twenty-five people in the audience when these guys played these coffee houses. But the music was as intense and meaningful as it has ever been. This is song is on the list as a nod to those coffee house days.

5. **1-2-5 – The Haunted**
In the 1960s, every city had a couple of hometown bands. Montreal had M.G. and The Escorts, JB and The Playboys, The Rabble, and these guys. The Haunted were dirty fuzzbox-playing bad boys. Guitars and drums mixed loud, vocals mixed back like The Kingsmen singing the forever-mysterious "Louie Louie". The Haunted's

only album is the Holy Grail for Canadian record collectors. I probably owned the single. There was a typo on the label of this big smash hit: they were called "The Hunted."

6. MON PAYS – Gilles Vigneault

I am not sure how it got by me, but it was while I was listening to the radio that I finally woke up to the fact and realized that there was more to Quebec than the little English neighbourhoods where I travelled. I feel silly saying that today, but in my defence, kind of the whole country was as surprised as me. And I know, living in Montreal, I should have had more of a clue, but you have to remember Montreal was pretty segregated back then. It was all very carefully organized. The English lived in the West End, the French in the East. Besides, the French hadn't really woken up to their existence either. So everyone was waking up in those days. And in Quebec, maybe the loudest alarm clock of all belonged to popular music. First came the *chansonniers*, icons like Félix Leclerc, Pauline Julien, and, of course, Gilles Vigneault.

7. LINDBERG – Robert Charlebois avec Louise Forestier

Suddenly, instead of playing cheesy covers of American hits, Montreal radio stations were playing original Quebec pop. And groups like Harmonium and Beau Dommage were good enough to cross over to English-Canadian audiences and even have some limited success touring in the States. It was very exciting to live in Montreal and have all this happening around you. And one of the most exciting stars in this exciting

scene was Robert Charlebois, who wore his Montreal Canadiens jersey to Paris and took the city by storm.

BACHMAN-TURNER OVERDRIVE

8. YOU AIN'T SEEN NOTHING YET – Bachman-Turner Overdrive

In the early 1970s, the CRTC enacted their controversial Canadian-content regulations: CanCon. The idea was meant to encourage and support the Canadian recording industry. Did it work? Oh yeah, it worked. A little piece of typically Canadian social engineering that served collective, rather than individual, rights and, I would put forward, the greater good. The proof of the pudding, as they say, is in the pudding eating. All of a sudden, Canadian musicians had an audience and, with an audience, a reason to stay in the business. Actually, for the first time, there was a business. In fact, before you knew it, there was the most unheard of thing ever: Canadian stars! I know, weird, isn't it? But there they were, not only being listened to at home, but around the world. Successful? None more so than this guy.

9. OPHELIA – The Band

These five guys who hail from small-town Ontario (or all but one of them) and who recorded two of the most acclaimed albums of the 1960s. Before they broke up, these guys were featured on the cover of *Time* magazine, for heaven's sake. Many

would say they changed the direction of popular music as much as anyone. I saw them in concert once: the early summer of 1969, Varsity Stadium, the Toronto Pop Festival. Sly and The Family Stone were the hit of the festival, as far as I was concerned, but these guys were there, and I saw them, and the mark they left on music was indelibly more permanent than the funky Family Stone.

10. A CASE OF YOU – Joni Mitchell

Blue may be my all-time favourite Canadian album ever. There hasn't been a decade in the last four that I haven't come back to this album over and over and over again. Heck, there hasn't been a month. The biting lyrics, the open-tuned guitar, the room full of flowers, the piano by the open window, the swaying dress, the cigarettes, the Greek island, the wind coming in from Africa. Oh, man, there isn't another album — a true tour de force. And so sardonically and cuttingly sung. "My love," says her lover, "is as constant as the northern star" . . . and without missing a beat, Joni lets loose the ultimate pop put-down, the break-up line of break-up lines. "Constantly in the darkness," she sings. "Where's that at? If you want me, I'll be in the bar." The best pop put-down anywhere. And when you hear her sing it and you imagine her sitting there, with her drink and her cigarette, sketching her map of Canada on her cocktail napkin, you want, with all your heart, to be the guy sitting on the stool beside her, smiling in the blue TV screen light.

51 Montréal -40°

Malajube

Dare To Care, 2006

"I think every Montrealer relates to '-40°'. It's painful and treacherous. This song makes the cold feel much more colourful and warmer in a funny way."

— Mikey Rishwain Bernard, M pour Montréal Festival

Indie rock took Canada by storm in the 2000s, led by artists such as Arcade Fire, Broken Social Scene, and Feist. It was no different in Quebec, and leading the way were Malajube, quickly tapped as the leader of a new Montreal sound.

Whatever that sound is, bass player Mathieu Cournoyer says it's not intentional: "I have problems to define what a Montreal sound is. I don't find much of a similarity between us or Wolf Parade or Arcade Fire. Maybe there's a vibe in Montreal, in the wintertime, not going out so much, and then it gets crazy in the summertime — when you can finally get out, that vibe is there. I don't know if it's like that in LA, you know."

Malajube's best-loved hit celebrates a side of Montreal most people normally don't appreciate: the weeks and weeks of cold weather. Cournoyer says singer/lyricist Julien Mineau meant it as a tribute: "He really loved the city, and loved how cold it was in the winter, people so dressed up, all the clothes, you couldn't even recognize your best friend if you walked past him."

Like much Quebec pop, there's an element of humour, too, with a memorable line about it being so cold, there was a polar bear taking the bus. The bubbly production matched the fun. "It's a happy song, it's the music," says Cournoyer. "When we started playing it, it made me feel good, the music fit with the lyrics, it's not too serious."

Malajube also broke new ground by bringing Québécois music to anglophone markets, only singing in French. "It's something I'm the most proud of since we started this project," beams Cournoyer. "When we stand back and look at it, we're just amazed that we're able to get our music out of Quebec. When we started, we were surprised to play Ottawa. Canada is supposed to be bilingual, but it's really hard to play French music in Hamilton or Edmonton. Hopefully we can keep doing that. It's certainly a lot better than it was ten years ago."

52 Cinnamon Girl

Neil Young

Reprise, 1969

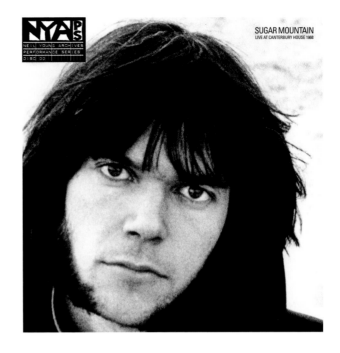

Neil Young's first, self-titled solo album was supposed to turn him into a star after leaving Buffalo Springfield. When the largely quiet disc failed, he had another plan, as he'd recently begun working with a band again. The re-christened Crazy Horse turned out to be excellent sparing partners, and the immediate result was some of the best electric songs of his career.

"Cinnamon Girl" is perhaps the best example of the partnership Young forged with ill-fated guitarist Danny Whitten. For this brief period in 1969, both live and on record, Whitten was the ultimate foil for Young. Unlike the fractious relationship he'd had with Stephen Stills, Young was able to count on Whitten to better his songs, without ego. Plus, they simply sound great together. The song is two-part harmony, from start to finish, Young going low and Whitten high, with Whitten's voice actually a bit louder and more pleasing. It's a wonderful touch, and there are precious few close-harmony, equal-brotherhood songs like it from guitar rock bands.

The interplay between Whitten's and Young's guitars is another part of the magic, the two so entwined it's hard to tell if there's one or two players. Over the years, the song has become a concert staple, with every drummer imitating Ralph Molina of Crazy Horse and his pounding 1-2-3-4 beat. Young uses it to rip out one of his most famous guitar solos. It was one of the highlights of the *Rust Never Sleeps* tour and live album, and often is used to peak crowd interest in the live set, a sure-bet classic that gets the audience excited. Sadly, though, since Whitten OD'd in 1972, the song has never been a full duet, as it was first conceived.

"Cinnamon Girl" gave Young only a modest hit on radio, but FM play was huge and the *Everybody Knows This Is Nowhere* disc, a big seller. Along with "Down By The River" and "Cowgirl In The Sand", Young now had a trio of guitar-powered classics that would serve him well for forty years.

> "You got a better one?"
>
> — Alan Wigney,
> *The Ottawa Sun*

53 You Oughta Know

Alanis Morissette

Maverick, 1995

"I still know every lyric and I'm sure all my girlfriends do, too."
— Meghan Gamble, Open Road Recordings

Pop music certainly has lots of female empowerment songs along its course. Nancy Sinatra's "These Boots Are Made For Walkin'" and Aretha Franklin's "Respect" pretty much said it straight. But there has never been one quite as bitter and angry as "You Oughta Know". Even though Morissette starts the song by claiming to be happy for her ex and his new girlfriend, that sentiment doesn't last past the first two lines. The rest of the song details just how pissed off and hurt she is, and pretty much skewers this pathetic and guilty former lover.

This guy — widely assumed, including by himself, to be actor Dave Coulier (Morissette has never chosen to confirm this) — is one of the most reviled males in history, thanks to the thirty-three million copies sold of her record-setting album. Morissette let it be known she was writing autobiographically. Her voice is full of venom, and the explicit lyrics and post-Grunge sound add to the overall angry tone.

Morissette's original, aggressive, and frank songwriting inspired an entire new brand of women performers. "You Oughta Know" spoke to young women like no other song had done. Maybe it was just time for some payback for all those bad break-ups many women have endured. Maybe Alanis was the first to say exactly what millions of women have wanted to say, in exactly that tone. Her ex gets called out for his deceitful behaviour, for his lies. Morissette says what many woman, and some men, feel when they are betrayed. In the end, she wins by having the sense and self-esteem to realize she shouldn't be the one to feel bad, and having the guts to tell him off, and tell the world about it.

It was quite an introduction to the new post-teen star Alanis in Canada, and an equally shocking debut in the rest of the world. She set sales records for female and debut albums, grabbed every trophy going in awards season, and *Jagged Little Pill* became the biggest-selling album in North America in the 1990s.

54 1234

Feist
Arts & Crafts, 2007

"Propelled a new generation of Canadian musicians, good to the Mac Apple core."

— Jelena Adzic, CBC-TV

If any song's success sums up the new order of the music world, it's that earned by "1234". It had everything going for it, and Feist rode a combination of new and old media to chart and sales heights. The song, rolled out in several media, was almost impossible to avoid. If you didn't hear it on radio or CD, it found you on TV or via the Internet.

It's as catchy as all get out, making great use of an old adage: keep it simple. It's almost shocking no one before had called a song "1234", the common count-in for most pop songs. It has the singalong quality of a nursery rhyme, and became an earworm song overnight, instantly memorable.

Then came the video, one of a new breed of clips that emphasize performance. It's a single, unedited shot for its three minutes and twenty-one seconds, Feist joined by dozens of dancers dressed in brilliant colours. The unique choreography made it a video everybody had to watch, so people sought it out on YouTube and other online sites, and the clip went viral.

The master stroke came with a commercial for the iPod. With this huge exposure, the song went from a modest hit to a smash. It was a synergy of cross-promotion, with the commercial itself an event for both the song and the product. People were buying iPods and downloading "1234".

The final touch of success occurred when it joined the select group of songs featured on the beloved *Sesame Street* show. With its "One two three four / Monsters walking 'cross the floor" version, Feist's appearance on the *Street* caused such a sensation that it was featured in every news outlet in the country. The clip with the Muppets became a hit, too, and has racked up 2.5 million views on YouTube.

The lesson "1234" taught the music business was that it's not about radio, or video, or TV, or CDs, or downloads, or videos, or websites. It's about all of them. It's a brand-new, multiplatform world.

55 Rebellion (Lies)

Arcade Fire

Merge, 2004

"Arcade Fire could be Canada's finest moment in music history."

— Eric Alper, E1 Distribution,

If you want to find out the reach of the Internet and how it has changed the way we find and enjoy music, look to the success of Arcade Fire. As of October 2009, the video for "Rebellion (Lies)" has been played over 2.5 million times on YouTube. Now, that's a hit single, and not based on any radio or video play or any sales charts.

"Rebellion (Lies)" is one of Win Butler's most interesting lyrics. Here, sleep is the enemy and dreams are the lies. His brother Will happens to be a poet with a degree in creative writing from Northwestern, so he's a good person to ask about the words. "'Rebellion' has always seemed aimed at the insomniac, to me," he says, "but maybe I'm too literal-minded."

Whatever the interpretation, it has a beat and you can dance to it, and sing along, too. That chant about the lies makes it a favourite for audience participation, and made it fun for the band, too, as they found ways to liven up the five-minute tune. "'Rebellion' probably has one too many sections to be ideally memorable," says Butler. "But that's true of every song over two and a half minutes. One of the band's favourite jokes, and it loses nigh on everything in the telling, is replacing the 'Lies! Lies!' falsetto part with 'Yeah! Yeah!' because it's the part that everybody in the crowd sings along to, and they sing whatever they want. Because the first rule is to be memorable — the part is memorable, the words are secondary, in the hierarchy of things. I mean, ideally, it all goes together."

That sums up Arcade Fire. There's the different name, the different backgrounds of the musicians originally from Canada, the United States, and Haiti, the many instruments and movements in each song, the special visual element of the videos and stage show, and the excitement of the live performances. Ideally, it does all go together to make something new and fresh.

56 Constant Craving

k.d. lang

Sire, 1992

"Songwriting perfection clearly meets unmatched delivery in this particular track."

— Tim Yerxa, executive director, The Playhouse

Not too many performers can successfully change their entire career with one song, but k.d. lang did just that with "Constant Craving". The former crazy country gal who had barnstormed into fame with a rockabilly/vintage Nashville sound was now an introspective, emotional balladeer. Her theatrics had been replaced with the wide acknowledgement that she was one of the top vocalists of the day, capable of holding her own with everyone from Tony Bennett to Roy Orbison.

Of course, the transition didn't happen overnight, but it is a textbook example of how to develop and mature as an artist, and not only bring along old fans but increase the audience at the same time. When lang broke out of Consort,

Alberta, she proclaimed herself the reincarnation of Patsy Cline. She ran on-stage at the Juno Awards in a wedding dress, hooked up with Cline's old producer, Owen Bradley, and recorded with old-guard stars Brenda Lee, Loretta Lynn, and Kitty Wells. So far, so country.

Slowly, lang dropped the more outrageous parts of her persona, instead focusing on her vocal skills. Her cover songs included vintage tearjerkers and her own, increasingly stronger material that emphasized her power and performance. Her most famous song to that point was her eye-opening duet on Orbison's "Crying", which introduced her to a much larger, mainstream audience, especially in the United States.

Still, her albums had been mostly

country. "Constant Craving", from *Ingenue*, dropped most of that sound and unveiled a new, mature lang. Her adult pop now flowed with the themes of the album: melancholia, desperation, unrequited love. Yet her voice gave listeners, and perhaps herself, the strength to pull through such hurt. It became her biggest hit, reaching the Top Forty and, more important, was a huge success on the adult contemporary chart. Formerly the home of mellow, middle-of-the-road artists from The Carpenters to The Captain & Tennille, the AC market now represented grown-up rock fans, and they bought her album in droves. lang had her new audience and career.

The twang was gone, but the torch remained.

57 Rockin' In The Free World

Neil Young

Reprise, 1989

"The first time I played this on stage was the first time I realized that I *needed* to rock out."

— Sarah Smith, musician, The Joys

While most of Young's best-loved songs date from his earliest years, this one snuck through as a later big favourite. It couldn't have come at a better time for the beleaguered star. By 1989, it looked like Young was a spent force. The eighties was a decade of drought for him, without one true hit record, sliding sales, and a confusing run of albums that had seen him change styles with every release. He'd tackled technology and isolation on *Trans*, doo-wop and rockabilly on *Everybody's Rockin'*, country on *Old Ways*, and by 1988, was working in soul-influenced horn music on *This Note's For You*.

All this confusion and experimentation might have been applauded if the albums had been at least artistically good, or challenging.

Aside from a handful of songs, they weren't. As fans have learned over the years, that's part of the beauty of Neil Young. You have to take his trial-and-error approach and stay with him for the long haul.

While he may be best known for beautiful and haunting acoustic numbers, his hard-core fans, and several generations of musicians and critics, love him best for his guitar anthems. Here, Young rolls out perhaps his heaviest sound ever, aided by his new rhythm section, Chad Cromwell on drums and Rick Rojas on bass. In a pounding opening, Young shreds and distorts the opening notes. Within a couple of years, they'd be calling this sound Grunge and hailing Young as the godfather of it. In live shows, the song

has become slower, louder, and even more powerful over the years, and as of 2009, had become a regular show closer or encore number. There's nothing quite like the lights going up in the chorus and seeing the thousands of fans jumping along, chanting the title phrase.

Usually, an acoustic offering from Young attracts more attention and success, but this electric track has so much fire, even the "Heart Of Gold" crowd was won over. Since "Rockin' In The Free World", Young's popularity has remained steady, and even occasional odd experiments are greeted with a smile. Fans know there's a good chance he'll amaze them next time.

58 Lovin' You Ain't Easy

Pagliaro

Much, 1971

"It was an honour to have him as a mentor. He's the king, the dark genius of Québécois rock music."

— Ivan Doroschuk, Men Without Hats

Memphis record producer Sam Phillips supposedly said if he could find a white boy who could sing R&B, he could make a fortune. Then Elvis Presley showed up at his Sun Studio. If there's an equivalent Canadian performer, it's Michel Pagliaro. The Montreal veteran of several sixties bands went solo in 1968, at first with a string of French hits. In 1971, he began recording in English as well, and became the first rock and roll artist to become a star on both sides of the linguistic divide.

English-language rock was already part of Pagliaro's repertoire, including recordings of "Hey Jude", "Wichita Lineman", and even "Na Na Hey Hey Kiss Him Goodbye". But his 1971 album *Pagliaro* saw him writing in English for the first time. It resulted in a big success, with hits "Lovin' You Ain't Easy", "Rainshowers", and "Some Sing, Some Dance".

At the same time, Pagliaro continued to work on his career in Quebec, and scored in 1972 what was to that time the biggest rock hit in the province's history, "J'entends frapper". Loved in both cultures, he became the first artist to win gold albums for both French and English albums, and his *Pagliaro Live* album was a truly bilingual triumph, featuring his hits in both languages.

"Lovin' You Ain't Easy" is a classic cut, an early piece of power pop. It features chiming guitars, thick harmonies, and a very familiar sound. Part of the album was done at London's Abbey Road, and Pagliaro certainly knew his Beatles. Montreal's Ralph Alfonso of the Bongo Beat label, and one of this book's jurors, describes Pagliaro as "singing like both John and Paul in two languages." You can hear that on "Lovin' You Ain't Easy", with its middle break classic nasally Lennon and its verses late-period McCartney or, more precisely, those of Beatles' proteges Badfinger.

1970s power pop is much loved by music collectors worldwide, who feast on the rich, melodic productions with just a whiff of the garage. Acts such as Big Star, The Raspberries, Dwight Twilley, Greg Kihn, and Badfinger are now revered for their sound. But far too few of the fans have heard "Lovin' You Ain't Easy", one of the best songs of its kind.

59 Lovers In A Dangerous Time

Bruce Cockburn

True North, 1984

"The crystallization of the blend of hooks, licks, and message that makes Cockburn so unique and special."

— Wilfred Langmaid, *The Daily Gleaner*

Bruce Cockburn songs can be tender-hearted or painful and dark, such as "If I Had A Rocket Launcher". This one captures both sides, with love and danger right in the title. There's usually a true story behind the words, and with "Lovers In A Dangerous Time", it's not an obvious one. Here's Cockburn to explain: "It was the early 1980s. I was living at College and Clinton in Toronto, the old Little Italy. My daughter would have been five, early school age. One day it struck me what awful prospects these kids must think they have. They were being taught all this stuff. In public school, her class, they bring in a pig's lung to show them what happens when you smoke. Stuff like that. I mean, that's okay for high school kids, but little kids — I didn't think should be treated that way. Of course, it made her a passionate anti-smoker. And at the time, my girlfriend and I were both smokers, so it led to some passionate discussions.

"I felt, if I were that age and aware of the world at that time, you look around and you'd go, you can't get close to somebody without worrying about AIDS, you've got environmental degradation, you've got war. All the same stuff we all had and every generation had, but more and more graphically and broadly communicated than was the case when I was a kid. It just seems to get worse and worse with each generation, and I was thinking about my daughter and her friends, these little kids in the playground, growing up in this world of stuff. So it was really motivated by a desire to communicate something encouraging to them."

"Lovers In A Dangerous Time" enjoyed a second life in 1991, when Barenaked Ladies made it their debut single. It was taken from the Cockburn tribute album, *Kick At The Darkness*, and Cockburn himself credits the cover with much of the ongoing popularity of the song.

60 Bobcaygeon

The Tragically Hip

Universal, 1998

"It comforts and makes you uneasy at the same time."

— Scott Chasty, Rock 94

One of the joys of listening to The Tragically Hip is following Gord Downie's lyrics, revelling in the flow of images and imagining what's behind the mystery. This is easier in some songs than in others, and Downie says "Bobcaygeon" has a basic story to follow: "Actually, I think this lyric might be one of my more linear ones, more straightforward than most. The video I made for it follows the lyrics pretty closely, using them as a kinda script. It all takes place in a twenty-four-hour period and goes in a big circle returning to the front porch it began on. There's this cop from the city and this girl from the country."

Okay, there's the story line, but

of course there's lots more going on in the song, as we find out our conflicted cop wants to get away from his job on horseback on Toronto's streets. There's a riot going on, outside and in his head. Downie's impassioned singing is one of his very best performances, supplying a flood of emotions for his character. Which ones, Gord? "Love, hope, reluctance, surrender, anger, contrast, tolerance, hate, doubt, forgiveness, fear: of evil-out-in-the-open-evil-just-under-the-surface, fear of loss (which Yoda would tell you is 'the path to the dark side') . . . and — you had me at 'love' — love, again."

Bobcaygeon is about a hundred

kilometres from Toronto, a perfect distance for someone who wants to get out of the city and perfect for Downie's song, as it rhymes with constellation. The story came to him during a stroll: "This lyric came together quickly walking home from ice cream along a leafy Toronto neighbourhood street, east end, June, warm evening around 7:30 pm." It's another in a long line of Canadian places and people that make their way into his lyrics. Downie says he's simply trying to relate, rather than fly the flag in his writing: "I like to think that people appreciate the human references in the songs."

61 A Case Of You/ California

Joni Mitchell

Reprise, 1971

> "'A Case Of You' never fails to give me goosebumps. It's the only love song I'll ever need."
>
> — Sofi Papamarko, music writer

There are several double-sided hits in this list of Top 100 Canadian singles, but this would be more accurately called a double-sided miss, if judged on chart placement alone. Neither song did particularly well in radio play or sales, but both received a significant number of votes in our poll, and have become long-time favourites of Mitchell fans.

Taken from the landmark *Blue* album, both songs feature Mitchell strumming her Appalachian dulcimer, with surprising chord choices and melodies that stretch from the bottom to the top of her considerable range. The simple backing allows us to stay riveted to the lyrics, as Mitchell famously opens up her heart.

"California" is far more light-hearted than other numbers on *Blue*, and serves as a travelogue about some of the places she visited on an extended European vacation before recording the album. She had retired from performing and recording for much of 1970, cancelling concerts and abandoning the Laurel Canyon lifestyle. Living in Los Angeles and being part of the new rock elite that included Crosby, Stills, Nash & Young had made her famous, but it had also made her feel isolated. The European trip, as well as one to Jamaica and Barbados, was to let her feel more in touch with people and to shed her celebrity.

"A Case Of You" is one of the best descriptions of the intensity of love any poet or songwriter has achieved. Using the religious metaphor of blood and holy wine, Mitchell sings to a lover who has truly touched her soul, and then delivers the key line: "I could drink a case of you / And still be on my feet." Almost forty years later, young (and not-so-young) women still use it as their Facebook status.

Along with "River", also from *Blue*, "A Case Of You" has become a modern standard, covered by such diverse artists as Prince, k.d. lang, and Diana Krall. Many, many bonus points are awarded to the song for its inclusion of the "I drew a map of Canada" line.

k.d. lang

One of the most successful and beloved singers and songwriters Canada has produced, lang has a deep appreciation of the great songwriters who have come from this country. In 2004, she paid tribute to some of them with the album *Hymns Of The 49th Parallel*, voted #59 in *The Top 100 Canadian Albums*. As a hit writer herself and one of the finest interpreters of pop songs working today, lang has significant insight into the quality of Canada's songwriters. Here she tells us why she made her tribute album to Canadian writers, and picks a few of her favourites.

"Two things were instrumental in making that record [*Hymns Of The 49th Parallel*]. One, making the American songbook with Tony Bennett (*A Wonderful World*, 2002). Experiencing those songs with somebody who helped create the American songbook really got me thinking about my country and the rich heritage we have in songwriting. And thinking how it's actually never been done, it hadn't really been done before, and thinking it was well overdue. Also, the political and emotional atmosphere of the States at that time, after 9/11 and the surprising and shocking election of George Bush, and how that, amongst my liberal peers, everyone was talking about moving to Canada, made me really appreciate my home. In that atmosphere, I couldn't find my own lyrical voice. I was really struggling with how to combat or deal with the environment, this emotional environment. And I really felt like turning to the Canadian poets was the best way, because, to me, they are hymns, they're spiritual, they transcend any sort of human construct of spirituality, and take it into the realm of music, and broad natural, environmental spirituality for me. I just felt like it was the right thing to do.

"Where do I start? Any Joni Mitchell song, any Neil Young song, any Leonard Cohen song, every Jane Siberry song. To me, Jane Siberry is one of the most underrated, overlooked songwriters in Canadian history. I love singing Jane Siberry songs, I wish I could do a whole record of Jane Siberry, which maybe someday I will. She didn't have the commercial success of the other people, but I think as a songwriter she's phenomenal. This deep sense of equanimity and compassion. She sees herself in everyone, and everyone in herself. When you come from a standpoint of that depth, I can't say enough about Jane Siberry."

62 New York City

The Demics

Ready, 1979

"Canada's singular original punk-era anthem."

— Bruce Mowat,
Audio-Video Sales

It's the classic story of a couple of British guys moving to the big city of London. Almost. Future Demics Keith Whittaker of Manchester and Iain Atkinson of Cambridge did move to London, only it was to London, Ontario. "Both of us emigrated at completely different times," says Iain (Atkinson) Staines. "We both went to the same high school. The guy had a lot of charisma, he was the real McCoy, that punk, in-your-face style. I had decided I was going to learn to play, and there was this punk rock thing going on, and maybe you don't have to play all that well. The only person I knew who would be ideal for that sort of role was Keith. He said 'Sure, why not?'"

There were precious few punk bands in Canada at the time and now exactly one in London. "We were the first to do it. From the very first show we did, it kind of exploded. It was packed to the rafters and people went completely berserk. I'm sure it was due to the charisma of Mr. Whittaker."

Staines says Whittaker, who died of cancer in 1996, was unique: "He was a really smart guy, but had a self-destructive streak. Even at the time, I was thinking that so many people were just a bunch of fucking posers, they were kids from the suburbs that were just jumping on the bandwagon, who didn't really have any hurt. Even though Keith acted like a yob beast and he drank, a lot of his inspiration was from books — he was so well read."

"New York City" may sound like a wish to escape to the big city, but it was actually a shot at some London rivals. "It was partially a piss take," says Staines. "There was another band in town, and all they would ever talk about was how wonderful New York was and how they had to get out as quickly as they can. I'm not sure if people get the irony of the song, but that's okay. 'Why is everything going to be so different anywhere else?' we thought. You can do it anywhere, and we did."

63 (Everything I Do) I Do It For You

Bryan Adams

A&M, 1991

"His ability to create a hook, even assembly line-like, is unequalled by any other Canadian songwriter before or since."

— Jaimie Vernon,
The Canadian Pop Music Encyclopedia

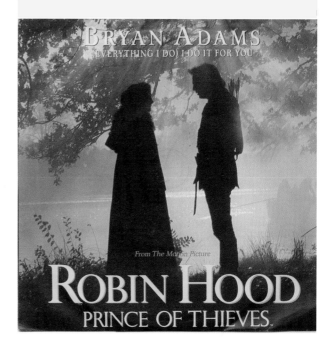

Bryan Adams had enjoyed lots of hits by this point in his career, but he was about to find out there was a secret club at the top of the tower of song. Written for the film *Robin Hood: Prince Of Thieves*, "(Everything I Do) I Do It For You" ultimately sold over ten million copies. Adams was now a truly international star.

Bob Mersereau: So, how big was it?

Bryan Adams: Apparently the world liked it. It was number one in any country that has a music chart in the world and has become one of the most recognizable songs of all time.

BM: Did you try to match it to the film, or did you choose instead to just write a great song?

BA: It was written specifically for the film and, of course, we wanted to make a great song no matter what. It took about forty-five minutes to write, and I wasn't sure after writing it if it wasn't too simple. In fact, I remember saying to my manager, if the song fails to connect, it's a good track for the album. One of the great things about this song's history is it came out before the film and was number one in the UK straightaway. So the song stood up without any hype. It stayed on the charts forever — in fact, I think it's still on the charts.

BM: Did you enjoy the process of writing for a film?

BA: Yes, very much. It was written by myself, Mutt Lange, and Michael Kamen, the composer of the soundtrack. It was the first of many songs the three of us wrote for films, and we were nominated twice for Oscars. I think if Michael had lived, who knows how many more we would have written together.

BM: Were you surprised that the song became such a success, and was it life changing?

BA: It was a monumental kick-off to my album *Waking Up The Neighbours* and a big part of the success of that album. There was a string of other songs that came after that from the same album, and we went from gigging in arenas to filling stadiums over the next five years.

64 Ahead By A Century

The Tragically Hip

MCA, 1996

In "Ahead By A Century", we're witnessing a stolen moment between two people. They're talking about something important between them, and then a hornet stings the singer. What's going on? We're not quite sure, nor are we meant to be fully enlightened.

In my discussions with lyricist Gord Downie, I remarked, "Often the songs don't seem to be big statements, they seem like stolen moments observed — just a frame of life, a glimpse of the story."

Downie replied, "And the memories of the stolen moments can seem stolen

"Beautiful and understated."

— Mark Logan,
Busted Flat Records

themselves, but, yeah, not the moon but the moon glinting off the gas pump at a truck stop in North Carolina. Not homesick but a thick-rimmed coffee mug and saucer. Not the tree, the tree fort. Not the betrayal, the apology. Not by a mile, but by a century — wait a minute — maybe there are big statements!"

So it's not just a flow of images, a piece of a conversation, with no beginning and end. Even if it's just a few moments, they are important ones. We can assume they're younger, because our singer thinks of "someday," and says it's not a dress rehearsal, this is our life. The big statement is that the other person is ahead of the singer, not by a mile, but by a century.

Now we're getting closer to the

story of those two people, and with a little more help from Downie, maybe we can understand exactly what's going on. So let's ask him directly: what's the story behind this song? "Disappointing you's getting me down" is his reply, quoting the lyrics directly. I think I get it. It's a couple, the singer is thinking of the future, but knows that the other person is greatly ahead of him. So he's a disappointment, and that's weighing too heavily on him.

Wow, there's a lot going on when you eavesdrop on two people in a tree. One last question remains. Ever been stung by a hornet, Gord, and if so, was it traumatic? "No, so . . . no."

65 5 Days In May

Blue Rodeo
Warner, 1993

"Keelor's guitar explodes across the night sky, raining down fireworks as Cuddy's vocals swell and waver like the northern lights."

— Will McGuirk, music writer

"5 Days In May" is one of the most powerful and emotional songs in the Blue Rodeo canon. Where "Try" set the tone for the start of the group's career, "5 Days In May" set up the next phase. For Jim Cuddy, it remains a milestone. "I certainly remember the writing of it. I was really into John Hiatt at the time, and I remember he said the most important line in any song is the first line. I thought that's a great piece of information, to make your first line have impact. That's when I came up with the line, 'They met in a hurricane / Standing in the shelter out of the rain.'

"I wanted to write this story, yet I wanted it to reflect things in my life. I wanted it to reflect the moment I met my wife. And I wanted it also to reflect this incident where, when we were in New Zealand, our soundman wrote his wife's name in the sand. I asked him what he was doing. He said he did that a lot, it was just something he did in every ocean he'd ever been to. I thought that was incredibly romantic, and I wanted to write it into a song. Those three things — I just started writing, and it was easy to figure out what I wanted to say. For me, it's such a template for what I write about: things that are attractive and surprise people, and then by the third verse you're wondering whether they stayed together or not."

Blue Rodeo now had a song that could match the emotional impact of "Try", plus the album *Five Days In July* became the group's bestseller. That's rare in a business that often sees the first single and album a band releases stay the fans' favourites. "The best thing for a career is to have a mid-career hit record," confirms Cuddy. "That record was so easy to make. Somehow there was a convergence of all the positive things in the band at that time."

66 I'm Movin' On

Hank Snow

RCA, 1950

"If he had plugged in, Hank would have been considered a rockabilly pioneer today."

— Roy Forbes "Bim", musician

Today's stars might want to stop and consider the popularity of Hank Snow. In a time way before mass celebrity culture and crossover chart success, Snow sold more than eighty-six million records, and "I'm Movin' On" went to number one on the US country charts for twenty-one weeks, a record that still holds.

One of country and western's biggest artists, Snow was really all East Coast. He was from tiny Brooklyn, Nova Scotia, and worked as a fisherman at age twelve. Snow became a big star in Canada first, signing to RCA Records in Montreal in 1936, recording dozens of songs, doing local radio shows and CBC broadcasts. He moved to the United States in the mid-

1940s, but stayed well connected to his home.

Graham Baker can testify to that. He lives in Blue Rocks, another place Snow once lived, close to Liverpool, Nova Scotia. As a kid, Baker began buying all his records. "Through the years, I got this big collection," says Baker. "Hank learned about it, and the next time he was in tour on the Maritimes, it was arranged for us to meet. He called me his friend, and I was honoured to be one."

Baker helped start a Hank Snow tribute concert, and The Friends of Hank Snow Society. This grew into The Hank Snow Museum and Country Music Centre, which opened in Liverpool in 1997. Baker is one of

the trustees and the resident Snow expert. With Snow's support, they collected a tremendous display of memorabilia, records, photos, his famous rhinestone-covered stage suits, and showpiece Cadillacs. "He was very generous and very honoured in us attempting this," says Baker. "He didn't insist on any first-hand control, but we had his blessings. He later said to me it was one of the highlights of his life to be honoured in such a fashion."

Sadly, he never got to see the museum. Snow died in 1999 in Nashville, where he'd lived since "I'm Movin' On" first hit. He'd gone from complete poverty in Nova Scotia to huge fame and riches, arguably the most successful music star in Canada's history.

67 Pour Un Instant

Harmonium

Polygram, 1974

"To me, Harmonium are a breath of freedom, peace, and joy, which absolutely represents our mentality here in Canada."

— Marion Brunelle, Live Jazz

Harmonium would feature orchestras and huge arrangements later in its career. But for their eponymous debut album, the band were all-acoustic, a trio featuring two guitars and bass, with some occasional drums and flourishes. "Pour un instant" was the big hit, introducing a sound influenced by modern folk and rock styles from outside Quebec, a melding that could only happen in that province.

Leader Serge Fiori, influenced by British progressive bands such as Genesis, had a taste for jazz often found in Montreal as well. Putting all these pieces together, Quebec had a new genre and a hugely popular group.

The trio of Fiori, Michel Normandeau (vocals and guitar), and Louis Valois (bass) had spent their formative days jamming at home, and

"Pour un instant" sounds much like that. It's just the two acoustics and bass, with Fiori adding a solo in the middle. The song reflects a whole host of styles but never quite fits into one, or copies another. The sweetly ringing guitars recall George Harrison, the dreamy lyrics echo the prog rockers, and the gentle vocals have the mellow vibe of the singer-songwriters. But with a little "yee-haa," it has that taste of Québécois energy as well.

There was a side benefit to all these influences from outside Quebec. College students in English Canada picked up on the band as well. Audiences from the Maritimes to British Columbia showed their appreciation for the music, even though the bulk of them couldn't understand the words. Harmonium

were able to tour across the country while not having to do separate material in English, as Robert Charlebois, Michel Pagliaro, or, later, Céline Dion would do.

Fiori has said that he and many of his generation were looking for their own music at the time, something that reflected the modern sounds they heard in Anglo rock but that retained a Quebec sensibility. "Pour un instant" stood out immediately, a new style of songwriting that pushed away the old-fashioned *chansonniers* and sounded just as fresh as the biggest English hits of the day.

68 Magic Carpet Ride

Steppenwolf
ABC-Dunhill, 1968

"What really stood out about this recording was the fact that Steppenwolf were excellent musicians and they got all their chops from the Toronto club scene."

— Andy Grigg, *Real Blues Magazine*

It's always difficult to follow up a blockbuster, especially one as definitive as "Born To Be Wild". That hit introduced Steppenwolf to the world, and changed hard rock forever. The next one would have to be a masterpiece, but somehow the band pulled it off. "Magic Carpet Ride" was almost as big a success, and proved the group were no one-hit wonder.

"Born To Be Wild" was written by band associate Mars Bonfire, but this time leader John Kay took the pen, along with bass player Rushton Moreve. Bonfire didn't get completely shut out, though. He was visiting the studio to show the group a new song and ended up playing rhythm guitar on the hit. There are actually two versions. The album take is much longer, and includes an experimental middle section where the group groove out on the riff and drop in some sound effects. The success of "Born To Be Wild" gave them extra leeway and a bigger budget in the studio. The spacey instrumental section was great for acid rock fans, but when it came to radio, it quickly got edited out, taking the single under the three-minute mark. It worked, with "Magic Carpet Ride" getting into the Top Five in Canada and the United States.

Pretty much everything released in the mid-to-late 1960s got accused of having some drug connotation, but the magic ride in this case had nothing to do with that, and everything to do with music. It refers to a new stereo system Kaye had bought with his "Born To Be Wild" money and placed in his bedroom. He could lie down on the bed and let the sound take him away.

Moreve didn't get to enjoy much of the success his song brought the band. He got fired soon after, when he refused to go back to California with the band for an appearance. His girlfriend, one Animal Huxley, had told him there was going to be an earthquake, with the sea swallowing California. Animal was the granddaughter of Aldous Huxley, the author of *Brave New World* and a noted LSD experimenter.

69 Money City Maniacs

Sloan

murderecords, 1998

"The siren starting the song brings a call to arms for anyone in a band, or dreaming of starting one."

— Eric Alper, E1 Distribution

The strength of Sloan lies in their unique partnership of songwriters. All four members contribute, and the songs can be created by any combination of the four, playing any number of instruments.

Patrick Pentland felt his way around the group for the first couple of albums. "With *Twice Removed*, I was confused about what we were trying to do as a band," he recalls. "The record was run by Chris and Jay and they had an agenda, which was try not to sound like *Smeared*. And I like *Smeared*. But by [third album] *One Chord To Another*, it was just do whatever we want."

Pentland became the hitmaker in the group. Singles "Everything You've Done Wrong", "The Good In Everyone", and "Money City Maniacs" were mostly his compositions. "I was getting pretty confident. We were concerned with keeping our fan base and keeping going. We were really trying for mainstream success at this time, not just alternative. We weren't afraid of mainstream either. We did the MuchMusic Video Awards and stuff. Remember when U2 stopped worrying about fame and went for it? We were in the same place. We figured why try to keep small, we wanted to be accepted."

For "Money City Maniacs", Pentland wanted a basic rock song, something easy to identify. "We had decided to embrace being a rock band.

We just wanted to play for fans. There are almost instructions for fans built in. It starts with a siren. It's an AC/DC thing, people will recognize it. We've got the clapping in the breakdown — oh my gosh, everybody's supposed to clap here."

Oh, and that memorable part about the guy covered in Coke fizz? It's a lesson on why you shouldn't read anything into lyrics. "Coke fizz just sounds cool, we never discussed it," Pentland says now. "There never was a practical joke or a guy covered in it. I didn't have a chorus for it, so Chris came up with a phonetic thing, the Coke fizz part, and it was cool; we didn't change it."

70 My Heart Will Go On

Céline Dion

Columbia, 1997

"This is what the world listens to."

— Bruce Mowat, Audio-Video Sales

Facts. You can argue about Céline Dion's singing style, choice of material, personality, showbiz glitz, and huge production as much as you want, and Lord knows most music fans either love her or hate her, but you can't deny the facts. "My Heart Will Go On" is simply one of the absolute most popular hit singles of all time, in sales, airplay, chart performance, or any other type of measurement you can choose.

It certainly didn't hurt that the big ballad was chosen as the theme song for James Cameron's blockbuster film *Titanic*, the first to earn a billion dollars in ticket sales worldwide. As audiences weeped their way out of the theatre, Dion's voice soared over the credits. With its eleven Academy Awards, everything associated with the movie was the craze of 1998, including Dion's lush love song. Like the film, it was a worldwide number one, perhaps an even bigger hit in Europe than in North America, and became one of the bestselling singles of all time, with more than ten million copies sold. It topped most Top Forty charts, as well as the adult contemporary surveys. It even became the number one Latin track in the United States, the first English-language song to do so, despite not having one bit of a Latin rhythm. It won its own Academy Award for Best Original Song, a Golden Globe, and then proceeded to take most other major music awards in most countries for record and single of the year, including four Grammy Awards. In Canada, the song helped spark Dion to five Junos in 1999, including the International Achievement Award.

"My Heart Will Go On" has become the most successful song of Céline Dion's unique career filled with hit singles sung in both French and English and record-setting stage shows in Las Vegas. And those are the facts.

Jay Ferguson & Chris Murphy

Here's an intriguing question: should band members have the same taste in music, or is it better for them to bring different influences to the sound? Maybe this exercise will help. Jay Ferguson and Chris Murphy, who both write songs for Sloan, were asked to name their favourite Canadian hits. They are two of the most fervent fans of pop music around. As you'll see, apart from The Guess Who, their lists are quite different, as Jay brings the sugar and Chris adds the spice.

JAY FERGUSON

1. **Joni Mitchell – FREE MAN IN PARIS**
Not about Canada, or a Canadian, but reminds me so much of being driven to preschool every day and hearing this hit on Top Forty radio in Nova Scotia. Super lyrics, cool riff, and sophisticated structure . . . but sounds so effortless. Did I mention Joni's one of the most underrated guitarists of all time?

2. **Pagliaro – LOVIN' YOU AIN'T EASY**
Canada's contribution to the category of greatest songs Paul McCartney didn't write.

3. **Ken Tobias – I JUST WANT TO MAKE MUSIC**
Another nostalgic hit for me. Underrated! When the strings come in on the second verse, it's one of the top five moments in Canadian rock history.

4. **Leonard Cohen – SUZANNE**
Chris will make fun of me for this. What do you say about a classic that everyone knows? Cool production? I dig the sharp lyrics and gentle mood combo.

5. **The Grapes Of Wrath – ALL THE THINGS I WASN'T**
My favourite of all their singles. So short and perfectly compact at just over two minutes.

6. **Joni Mitchell – RAISED ON ROBBERY**
I know . . . Joni again. Her grooviest song. Fun, unwinding storyteller lyrics over a musical runaway train with a dash of

Canadiana. Oh . . . and saxophone soloing, for those interested.

7. **Neil Young – CINNAMON GIRL**
Even if it was just the handclaps and the riff repeated, it might still make this list.

8. **Nelly Furtado – I'M LIKE A BIRD**
I guess I'm a sucker for those hits with good melancholy (but not sappy, though!) lyrics and a big chorus. This one still holds up. Kind of a secret favourite. The mellotron is a nice bonus.

9. **The Guess Who – SHAKIN' ALL OVER**
Best version of this song! Ever! A good case for the argument that rock and roll production did not need to progress beyond 1965.

10. **Zumpano – THE ONLY REASON UNDER THE SUN**
We released this 7" single on our murderecords label back in the late 1990s. I was a fan and we asked them for a song to release. We didn't know what we would receive, but I was so pleased with what they sent that I listened to it ten times in a row immediately upon arrival. Really excellent song.

CHRIS MURPHY

1. **The Guess Who – NO SUGAR TONIGHT/ NEW MOTHER NATURE**
Canada's Lennon/McCartney make two songs from one chord progression.

2. **The Poppy Family – WHERE EVIL GROWS**
This song scared the hell out of me as a kid.

3. **April Wine – BAD SIDE OF THE MOON**
Elton John may have written it but this bass line rules.

4. **Trooper – RAISE A LITTLE HELL**
I believe I substituted hell with heck around my parents.

5. **Rush – THE SPIRIT OF RADIO**
No one touches Rush . . .

6. **Rush – TOM SAWYER**
. . . during this period.

7. **Payola\$ – EYES OF A STRANGER**
I like the one truncated "eyes of a stranger." Crafty.

8. **Platinum Blonde – IT DOESN'T REALLY MATTER**
Having their first EP before the LP came out made you cool in my school.

9. **The Pursuit Of Happiness – I'M AN ADULT NOW**
I think of this as the cooler older brother to my song "Underwhelmed".

10. **Tegan and Sara – WALKING WITH A GHOST**
I'm a sucker for subtle chord changes under the same melody line and for saving something for the end of the song. I wish the lyric was "please don't exist" instead of "please don't insist." No one asked me.

71 Crabbuckit

k-os

Astralwerks, 2004

With a MuchMusic Video Award for Best Pop Video and a Juno for Single of the Year, "Crabbuckit" is one of the most successful hip-hop songs in Canadian music history. The outspoken artist, whose *Joyful Rebellion* album included several swipes at the state of the music business and hip-hop attitudes, plays that card rather subtly on this insanely catchy number.

Based around a marching, stomp-clap beat, acoustic guitar, tambourine, two-note piano, and a very old-school sax, "Crabbuckit" caught on, thanks to a great melody, infectious rhythm, and a unique lyric. k-os is singing about the crab mentality, a phrase used to describe when, out of jealousy or resentment, people try to tear down someone who is rising above the rest of the group. Crabs will pull down any of their fellows that try to escape the bucket. k-os is talking about his struggle, saying "no time to get down 'cause I'm moving up."

That heavy message aside, it was simply a fun song and video. It spoke to lots of Torontonians, with k-os naming Yonge Street in the first verse and pacing down recognizable city streets in the video. Familiar TTC streetcars pass behind. The fun continues as k-os slips on a special set of sunglasses that let him see who is real and who the crabs are. There are lots of crab-people, but they can't slow him down or stop him from an impromptu jam session with Nelly Furtado, who just happens to be hanging out in front of the club k-os is heading to. And the rap at the end of the song finishes with a shout-out to The Tragically Hip. This groove just screams, "O Canada."

While generally placed in hip-hop, k-os incorporates anything and everything into his music, appealing to rap fans, alternative rock audiences, and dance floor habitués. The all-round musicality of "Crabbuckit" announced that he couldn't be forced into one place and was going to climb over all the crabs out there.

72 This Beat Goes On/ Switchin' To Glide

The Kings

Elektra, 1980

Bar band veterans of the 1970s, The Kings had more than paid their dues gigging all over southern Ontario. Recording was the next move. "We had saved up some dough and went into the best studio in Toronto," says guitar player Mister Zero. "Nimbus 9 was where Jack Richardson had recorded The Guess Who and Bob Ezrin had done Alice Cooper. We knew the history, but we didn't know Bob was around. He was back after doing *The Wall* with Pink Floyd. One of our managers got to talking with him, and he took our tapes home to listen. His kids liked our stuff and so did he. So it was a Cinderella story when he went to Elektra in LA and got us a deal."

The key track was a lengthy medley of two songs, "Switchin'

"The ultimate mating call for weekend party-itis."

— Lisa Millar, music consultant

To Glide" and "This Beat Goes On". "We wrote them separately but they both seemed incomplete," remembers Zero. "So we tried to find a way to combine them musically and lyrically. Then the magic started to happen."

At over six minutes, the song faced the usual tough battle to get radio play. It was first released in an edited version, as just "Switchin' To Glide". It was a modest hit, but a few stations opted for the longer version. Zero says, "That is when the phones started ringing at radio stations all over the US and Canada — 'What was that weird thing we just heard?'

We pushed for it, as did Bob and our management, and it worked!"

In the space of a few months, The Kings had gone from the bar circuit to touring with Jeff Beck, The Beach Boys, and Eric Clapton, and appearing on *American Bandstand*. It was a case of being in the right place at the right time with the right song, and working long and hard: "Last week I got an email from a guy in New Hampshire who had never heard it, just thought it was some awesome new song that in his mind stuck out from all the stuff he was currently hearing. It still sounds that fresh."

73 Old Man/The Needle And The Damage Done

Neil Young

Reprise, 1972

From his landmark *Harvest* album, these two tracks rival "Heart Of Gold" as the most popular acoustic-based songs of Young's career. Released as the follow-up to that number one hit, "Old Man" snuck into the Top Forty in the United States, but in Canada it was a huge hit, making the Top Ten.

about their being much the same, needing someone to love them. Avila's wife also worked and lived on the ranch as a caretaker. As in two other key *Harvest* tracks, "Heart Of Gold" and "A Man Needs A Maid", Young admits to this near desperation to be loved, calling his new ranch a paradise that makes him think of two. As with

"The Needle And The Damage Done" is Young's famous response to the rampant heroin use he'd seen in the rock world. As he describes on the Archives Series concert release *Live At Massey Hall 1971*, he didn't write it about the stars, he wrote it for the many good musicians who didn't come to fame because of their addiction. The song is actually a live recording, taped at a UCLA show eleven days after he played the Massey Hall gig in Toronto. This started a pattern where Young would use live recordings on his discs, often with the crowd noise removed, and certainly "The Needle And The Damage Done" is perfect in this performance. Though never a charting single, this B-side received so many votes in this book's poll that it had to be included in the Top 100.

"A song about wisdom written by a young Canadian in his twenties."

— Craig Martin, founder, Classic Albums Live

While initial speculation was that the old man was his famous father, journalist Scott Young, Neil has set the record straight since. It's actually one Louis Avala, who was the caretaker of his newly purchased Broken Arrow Ranch in California. Conversations with Avila led to the crucial lines

"Heart Of Gold", Linda Ronstadt provides the memorable harmonies, and James Taylor adds the banjo. Original *Harvest* pedal steel player Ben Keith was a fixture in Young's touring group from 2007 until his death in 2010. "Old Man" gets an airing at most shows.

Joel Plaskett

Plaskett hit the ground running, forming Thrush Hermit in 1992, and he hasn't stopped since. The beloved Nova Scotia group made one of the great Canadian alternative records of all time, *Clayton Park*, voted #85 in *The Top 100 Canadian Albums*. After Thrush Hermit broke up in 1999, he continued solo and with The Joel Plaskett Emergency. Along the way, he's rewritten the record books for most wins at the East Coast Music Awards, produced several albums, and started his own record label. In 2010, he even reformed the Hermit for a series of live shows and a retrospective boxed set. He slowed down enough to jot down his favourite eleven Canadian hits.

1. **FREE MAN IN PARIS – Joni Mitchell**
   I've read this song is about David Geffen. Lucky man. Who else can write a hit song with the word "unfettered" in the chorus? She's the top.

2. **UNDERWHELMED – Sloan**
   Sloan rocked my world. I heard the four-track demo of this tune and saw them play it at their second show. This song single-handedly changed the way I felt about the purpose of lyrics. Funny and heartfelt, with references for Nova Scotians (like "the LC" — Liquor Commission).

3. **OH LONESOME ME – Neil Young**
   You know you're cool when the first single from a record as great as *After The Gold Rush* is a cover of a Don Gibson tune. Neil's version is beautiful.

4. **SCRATCHES AND NEEDLES – The Nils**
   I heard this on CKDU when I was fourteen and it took me three years to find out who it was! Mystery rules . . . screw the Internet! The true beginnings of melodic punk rock from Canada.

5. **IT MAKES NO DIFFERENCE – The Band**
   Melodic perfection, and Rick Danko's voice breaks my heart.

THE BAND

6. **LETTER FROM AN OCCUPANT – The New Pornographers**
   I don't really know what the lyrics mean but the melody is unreal. The energy in this song could power Dartmouth for a couple months.

7. **SUMMER SIDE OF LIFE – Gordon Lightfoot**
   I love the way this sounds and feels. It's like it has these dark corners to discover on every listen. The harmonies are epic and the words are amazing.

8. **SNOWBIRD – Gene MacLellan**
   Perfect.

9. **BOBCAYGEON – The Tragically Hip**
   I really fell for this song after watching The Hip play it every night when we toured with them. Gord Downie's imagery is so strong and this one pushes all the right buttons.

GENE MacLELLAN

10. **HEY THAT'S NO WAY TO SAY GOODBYE – Leonard Cohen**
    My favourite Cohen song. Just right for the night.

11. **LET THERE BE DRUMS – The Incredible Bongo Band**
    This rocks! It was the theme for Atlantic Grand Prix Wrestling in the eighties. I loved that show. The Cuban Assassin!

74 1990

Jean Leloup
Audiogram, 1991

"Qui de mieux que Jean Leloup pour décrire '1990', plonge dans la guerre du Golfe, en texte absolument délectable!"
– Marie Lefebvre, RockDétente 102.7

At the start of the nineties, Jean the Wolf had Quebec dancing with joy. But what topics! "1990" concerned spiralling technology, corporate globalization, weapons of mass destruction, and the first war in Iraq. Oh yeah, and then it ended with Leloup comparing his sexual abilities to the Gulf War. Boogie on, Jean.

Those are big issues, but they are delivered with equal doses of humour and irony, which are usually avoided at all costs in the English pop world. Or, if such themes are tackled, it certainly isn't over a dance track. Such is the talent of the controversial bad boy of Quebec pop. Jean Leloup stirs things up and has been a restless talent throughout his career, carrying out a hit-and-run campaign on popular culture. He's disappeared for years at a time, re-emerged with film or book projects, buried the Leloup name, and resurrected it in grand spectacles.

Certainly, his greatest success was this chart topper, which hit like an explosion, first in Quebec and then in Europe. The 1990 version of Jean Leloup was almost a cult figure. The bad boy persona was pushed forward with the provocative lyrics, flashy clothes, even a top hat. He was an image of elegant decadence, wallowing in art. Of course, it was an act, following in the Quebec pop tradition of Robert Charlebois. Leloup had proven to be a chameleon in the same class as David Bowie, unveiling new looks and concepts with each new project.

Unlike the bulk of English artists, Leloup also felt comfortable moving from one style to the next. His 1989 hit "Printemps-été" was rockabilly poetry, and in the past he'd mined his youth in Togo with some African rhythms. Later work would see him turn into a guitar-loving singer-songwriter. Quebec audiences do seem more open to such musical wandering, something that has killed many an English group. And dabbling in disco is still a no-no for many North American rock fans. But Jean Leloup proved he can write a song about death, taxes, war, and sex, and have a whole culture hit the dance floor.

75 Eyes Of A Stranger

Payola$

A&M, 1982

A huge hit, "Eyes Of A Stranger" won a Juno for Single of the Year. It was moody, mysterious, and had an exotic reggae feel. So, what was the mystery behind those eyes?

"I said to myself, what would be the most ridiculous thing you would say to a woman?" recalls Paul Hyde. "And it was 'Can I touch you to see if you're real?' And then it went from there. I came up with the world's worst pick-up line, and then some other not-so-great lines, but somehow they work. The public didn't seem to mind."

Cheesy pick-up lines aside, "Eyes" propelled the Vancouver group to success. The band were anchored by the partnership of Hyde and Bob Rock, who met as teens on Vancouver Island. Hyde usually wrote the words after Rock brought the music, as was the case with "Eyes Of A Stranger".

"Bob's told me he didn't even think it would get any airplay," says Hyde. "He thought it was too reggae sounding. I thought it was good, but when we started playing it at gigs before it was recorded, people started coming up to us saying, 'Hey, that "Eyes" thing is a good song.' And we realized this was going to be popular. We certainly didn't write it to be popular, there wasn't a lot of reggae on the radio at that time — it got better with The Police later on."

One of the keys was the producer, former Bowie guitarist Mick Ronson.

"He just happened to walk into A&M at the same time," says Hyde, "saying, 'Hey, have you got anybody that needs producing?' It was a great thing for me and Bob, with one of our heroes

> "With its ominous tone, lyrical paranoia, and hypnotic reggae beat, 'Eyes Of A Stranger' instantly reeled me in."
>
> — Kevin "Sipreano" Howes, producer/manager/deejay

producing us. Very talented, and just the nicest guy you'd want to meet."

Rock would become one of the world's top producers himself, with Metallica, Aerosmith, and many more. Their music partnership has never ended, and even the Payola$ name was brought back in the mid-2000s, with Hyde confirming that as of 2009 a new album has been recorded.

76 Hasn't Hit Me Yet

Blue Rodeo

Warner, 1993

Blue Rodeo's *Five Days In July* album included a number of surprises, including a role reversal for the group's songwriters. Jim Cuddy had brought in the moody, lengthy track "5 Days In May", while Greg Keelor been listening to a lot of Ian & Sylvia, and that was what was getting him going. I think this was a result of him absorbing this folk-rock-poet style. As usual with Greg, it was fiercely honest about his situation at the time.

"Cold December nights, sunsets, and Lake Ontario."

— Darin Clark, Z99

had the shorter, upbeat singalong number in "Hasn't Hit Me Yet". Even Jim Cuddy didn't see that coming: "I guess it's the flip side to '5 Days'. It was a very tightly arranged song, a bit folk-rock. It was very interesting for Greg to bring that in. Greg sometimes surprises me with the styles he's into on each record. I think that Greg had

I remember hearing that for the first time and thinking, holy fuck, this is going to be good."

The song, and parent album, heralded a new era for the group. There were new group members, and new instruments that would define the different sound. "It was a way for us to try to figure out how we were

going to use the pedal steel," says Cuddy of the sessions. "It was a way for us to imagine what kind of band are we now. We had added it on *Lost Together*, to be a countrified version, and now we had to figure out how to keep it in there for good. The folk-rock thing worked."

Country, folk-rock, rock — for once in music, the labels didn't seem to matter for the crowds. Whatever Blue Rodeo threw at them, audiences returned it with love, including "Hasn't Hit Me Yet". "It was fun to play, and it has been one of those songs that I love playing live," says Cuddy. "It just gets everybody going. You love to see those songs when people throw their heads back. They always sing that chorus, 'Hey, hey, it hasn't hit me yet.'"

77 You Ain't Seen Nothin' Yet

Bachman-Turner Overdrive

Mercury, 1974

Tsk tsk. Mocking his brother's stutter. That's what Randy Bachman was up to when he sang b-b-b-baby on "You Ain't Seen Nothin' Yet".

Like all big brothers, he'd been picking on Gary Bachman since they were kids. He recorded the stutter in the studio, to send to Gary as a joke. He was pretty horrified when the band wanted to keep it. "True," he admits, "this song was not intended to be released and was against all my protests, but it went to number one in over twenty countries and was BTO's only million-selling single, as we were basically an album band."

They *were* an album band, but had recently tasted pop success with "Takin' Care Of Business", a Top Ten hit in the United States and Canada. Bachman might have moulded the group in a heavier style than The Guess Who, but he wasn't against pop hits either. "Are you kidding?" he responds, when asked if getting back to number one was important to him.

"B-b-b-baby."

— Mark Logan,
Busted Flat Records

"I was thrilled. That wasn't my target when I started out, but it came to that, and I was amazed. I had written the songs, I had played on the songs, and with BTO, I sang and produced the songs. This was a big accomplishment for me and I'm totally amazed and proud of it."

It was Bachman's singular drive that had taken him back to the top of the rock world. Since he had started playing in bands in the early 1960s in Winnipeg, he had really only enjoyed a short period of success with The Guess Who from 1968 to 1970. All those years had been spent on the road, playing teen clubs, bars, curling rinks, and one-nighters. It was a mental and physical grind, especially for a sensitive tea-totaller: "Rock was my life. I knew it, and that what I was born to do. Nothing could ever or will ever stop me. Always moving, like a shark. Gotta keep the rock rollin'.

"I have the same drive as always. My passions are relentless. I love what I do and am so thrilled to make a living at doing it."

78 Wondering Where The Lions Are

Bruce Cockburn

True North, 1979

"The simple opening guitar line never fails to bring a smile to my face, and after thirty years, it's a song I've never tired of."

— John Threlfall, music writer

In 1979, Bruce Cockburn surprised his audience with an actual hit song in Canada and the United States. "Wondering Where The Lions Are" had a Jamaican feel and featured Toronto reggae singer Leroy Sibbles's band. "I felt I should get Jamaican guys to play it," he remembers. "There's such a long and tawdry history of white people playing black people's music and not putting any black people in it, misappropriating it. I didn't want to be guilty of that."

With its infectious rhythm, "Wondering" had audiences singing along and smiling. All the time, Cockburn was having his own chuckle, since he knew what was really going on in the lyrics. "Everybody dies!" he reveals. "And it's all over the place. Nature's dying, the river's dried up, there are soldiers marching."

It hardly matches the tune, but here is what set the song in motion: "I was having dinner with someone I knew who was very high up in the security establishment, the Cold War espionage thing, monitoring of electronic transmissions. He couldn't say much of anything about his work, of course. At the time, China and Russia were sort of coming to blows along their mutual border. He said this was very worrisome because we had a deal with the Russians, an understanding that neither side was going to surprise the other, that if we're going to do something we'll let you know first, or they'd just keep leaking enough information that each side has a sense of the other's inclinations and capacities. But China wasn't part of that. China might have had nukes, and nobody knew how far along they were in having a way to deliver those nukes and what their attitude was toward using them. And he said, over dinner, 'For all we know we could wake up tomorrow and it would be the end of the world.' So I woke up the next morning, the sun was shining, the world was still there, and that's where the first verse came from."

And you thought it was about lions.

79 You Could Have Been A Lady

April Wine

Aquarius, 1972

"It was the double guitars, man, and that grinding hook . . .
I just couldn't get enough of it."

— Doc Halen, CHEZ

April Wine celebrated their fortieth anniversary in 2009. Group members have written a long list of hit singles, but back in the early days, April Wine were best known for their covers. "You Could Have Been A Lady" is now so connected with the group that most fans don't even realize it was picked up from a hot band in England. Brian Greenway plays guitar for the group: "Ralph Murphy, who produced the first April Wine singles and albums, was the one who brought it to the band, the same as Elton John's 'Bad Side Of The Moon' [their next single, also a Canadian hit]. He had his ear tuned in."

The song was from the group Hot Chocolate, also the writers of the song "Brother Louie", a seventies hit for Stories in North America. That group would have to wait until the mid-seventies for North American fame, with the disco hit "You Sexy Thing". In the meantime, April Wine radically reworked "You Could Have Been A Lady" to Canadian fame.

Greenway says that, despite the song's age, it's still April Wine's most popular number in Canada. "There's not a show where we have not played it, one of those things that you have to play. It's usually in the encore, or towards the end of the show, as it's a real pick-me-up. Everybody knows it right away, as soon as that first guitar chord goes duh-de-de-dah — it's almost like a Bo Diddley thing —

and everybody goes YAHHHH! Hands go in the air, fingers go up, all the guys drinking beer go, woah! It's a real anthem for those people. It's all across the board, young and old. Even though the song is way older than some of the people listening to it, they just love it."

That's Canada. How does it go over in England? "We weren't playing that tune when we played there," says Greenway. "It was during the *Nature Of The Beast* days, and they had us billed as a heavy metal band."

80 Something On My Mind/Let's Shake

Teenage Head

Attic, 1980

"Why? Coz nobody puts Frankie Venom in the corner."

— Lisa Millar, music consultant

When you bought a single on a 45 rpm record, you always got a bonus. There was something on the other side, the B-side. Often, these were throwaway songs or a track from the latest album. On rare occasions, you'd find a treasure. Rarer still, sometimes the disc jockeys would like a B-side so much, they'd start playing that. Only a very few times would both sides of the record become Top Forty hits.

Teenage Head's Gord Lewis was a huge music fan growing up, and knew all about this special achievement. Then, it happened with "Something On My Mind"/"Picture My Face". "I look back at it as being

quite a honour," he says. "I remember thinking that this is reserved for Creedence Clearwater Revival, The Beatles, bands like that. Wow. I watched the charts as a kid, so I knew these double-sided hits didn't happen too often."

Teenage Head had become the country's top punk band, although that wasn't scaling too high a peak. Radio, retailers, and record labels were still resisting the loud and aggressive sounds, and most venues didn't want the bands either. Teenage Head had always had a soft spot, though. "It was originally called 'Just A Friend'," says Lewis. "Frank [Venom, lead singer] had written

it about a woman he knew, a nice sincere song about somebody that was close to all of us. It was the soft side of him that people didn't know about. He had incredible heart, an enormous heart, so that does come out in that song."

That gave Top Forty stations something to play, but for the more adventurous ones, there was a tune on the B-side that would become the band's definitive statement, "Let's Shake". "That's Teenage Head's signature song," Lewis confirms. "That's still the crowd pleaser. I think it's the rhythm, it's the chord progression, it's a very rock 'n' roll song. Lyrically, it's right to the point, being able to say something in two words and get the point across."

81 Help Me

Joni Mitchell

Asylum, 1974

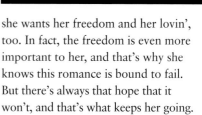
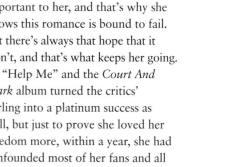

"Before punk and disco, this was the sound of the seventies. Yet, in any decade, it could only have sounded exactly the way Mitchell recorded it."

— Mark Rheaume, CBC Radio

Joni Mitchell has always had an uneasy relationship with fame and success, but for a couple of years in the 1970s, she found herself making music that sprang up the charts. The mix of her heart-grabbing songwriting, a new jazz flavour, and more confidence made "Help Me" a Top Ten hit, the biggest of her career.

It was quite the change from the folk-based Mitchell that fans had come to know. Just three years before, she'd made her most acclaimed album, *Blue*, largely on acoustic guitar and dulcimer. Now, she had Tom Scott blowing sweet sax along with a full set of LA session aces.

Regarded as the most confessional of the singer-songwriters, on "Help Me," Mitchell was still singing about love, but now it was almost joyful, with a hint of danger. She loves that crazy feeling, loves being in love, but knows she's getting in trouble again. Yet the music tells us, and her, to forget that it's a mistake — go with the excitement. There was no room for her blue side in this song. Even as she calls out for help, she doesn't really want us to stop her diving in heart first.

She's not helpless or blameless in this affair. While she knows the guy is a "sweet-talking ladies' man," she admits to being a flirt and, like him, she wants her freedom and her lovin', too. In fact, the freedom is even more important to her, and that's why she knows this romance is bound to fail. But there's always that hope that it won't, and that's what keeps her going.

"Help Me" and the *Court And Spark* album turned the critics' darling into a platinum success as well, but just to prove she loved her freedom more, within a year, she had confounded most of her fans and all the deejays with the jazz and world rhythms of *The Hissing Of Summer Lawns*. Much like Neil Young, who wilfully destroyed his Top Forty career after "Heart Of Gold", Mitchell followed her muse, not her bank account.

82 We're Here For A Good Time (Not A Long Time)

Trooper
MCA, 1977

"This song makes me feel like living for the moment."

— Sarah Smith, musician, The Joys

"A very good friend of mine told me something the other day." That's a simple sentence, something we can easily understand and to which we can all relate. It's also a true story — it really happened that way to Trooper's Ra McGuire, and it's the opening line of a Canadian classic. "We were rehearsing the *Knock 'Em Dead Kid* album and the session was looming," says McGuire, picking up the story. "As we left one of the final rehearsals, I was freaking out a bit about having enough good songs for the record. A very good friend, Greg Skaaravik, put his arm around me in the parking lot after the rehearsal.

Guess what he said to me? I wrote all the lyrics for the song the next day, sitting on a log on [Vancouver's] Kits Beach."

By the time the band started working on the new set of lyrics, McGuire knew he had tapped into something: "'Good Time' is one of the very few songs that I knew would be a hit as soon as the arrangement came together in rehearsals. I couldn't get it out of my head." It was the kind of songwriting McGuire always hopes to accomplish. "I'm sure every lyricist would like to believe that their words are connecting, in a visceral way, with the people listening to the song. I try

to write words that either are true or feel true . . . and that don't suck. I have varying degrees of success with that."

Between Greg's advice and McGuire's lyrics, Trooper managed to come up with a hit, and to sneak a subtle piece of philosophy into Canada's clubs as well. "We reprise 'Good Time' at the end of our set," says McGuire. "Lately, I've been considering making that one a weightier version that amplifies the reasonably important idea that we only do this life thing once and it's up to us how we do it."

Trooper's heavier than you thought.

83 Sunny Days

Lighthouse

GRT, 1972

The trouble with a hit record is that you immediately become busier than ever. After the success of "One Fine Morning", Lighthouse were in great demand on the road, plus another hit single was in order. "We had been out touring for a solid six months," remembers drummer Skip Prokop. "We were going to come off the road, we were going to take a vacation."

At least, that was the plan. Skip Prokop was going back to Mississauga, grab the family, and head up to cottage country. As bandleader and chief songwriter, he had to stop by the office one last time when the tour wrapped up. "So everybody's geared up for the vacation," says Prokop. "I get down to New York and Jimmy [Ienner, producer] says, 'You know what, Skip? Maybe the rest of the

"The ultimate ode to the joys of summer."

— Ian Scott, music writer

band is going on vacation, but you're going home and you better write some hits.' He says, 'There's great material here, but I don't hear the song that's going to explode.'

"I go home, and let me tell ya, I did not win father-of-the-year award that week. All the stuff's packed, fishing rods, you name it, and I say, 'We're not going, I gotta write.' At that point, that particular week, we got into an incredible heat wave for about five days, and it was just brutal. We didn't go away to a cottage or boating or anything."

At that point, Prokop got so

desperate, he went out and bought a kiddie pool. "It was so damn hot, I picked up one of those little square metal frameworks with little feet on each corner, and it has an apron kind of pool — you just slip the bars through and fill it up with water for the kids. And I was sitting out there, it was so hot, I had a beer, and I was sitting on the edge with my guitar, and I wrote 'Sunny Days'."

It was the best family vacation they never took, and no doubt paid for many others over the years.

84 Le petit roi

Jean-Pierre Ferland

Barclay, 1970

"He is one of the most popular Quebec singers of all time, and this song has a nice melody and beautiful lyrics."

— Marie Lefebvre, RockDétente, 102.7

The album was *Jeune*, a breakthrough in Quebec music. It marked a couple of major developments. First, Ferland was a successful *chansonnier* of the old school, romantic and expressive, poetic and personal. With this disc, he would bring that style into the modern music world, creating a concept piece with rock instruments, an orchestra, studio effects, and humour. Second, it was a major recording at Studio André Perry in Montreal, proving Quebec and Canada had entered the world of high-quality production, on a par with London, New York, and Los Angeles.

Its lead single was "Le petit roi" — the little king. Instead of the acoustics that had accompanied his ballads of the past, this time Ferland's song opened with piano and electric bass, joined by drums and rock rhythm guitar, then fluttering strings, subtle horns, and backing vocalists, layered with some studio trickery. It was catchy, sophisticated, and, best of all, sounded great. While it retained enough of the old *chansonnier* style for that audience, it clearly courted the next generation of Québécois, fresh from the Quiet Revolution, who were looking for a modern and unique artistic voice.

Ferland retained the lyric style that had brought him to fame, writing an emotional, personal story, admitting some faults and allowing his audience to see his flaws but to warm to him. Here, at first, he remembers how he was as the little prince, reigning in his personal kingdom. But that led to juvenile turmoil. Now he feels reborn. He's come through the problems of youth and feels he has a handle on his life, but he must leave his past behind. It's a tender and melancholy song, as we shed a tear, yet smile for the singer. He's now the little king, all grown up. Or, as the singers gently taunt him, "Hey gumball, what are you, a man now?" Okay, it loses something in the translation. It sounds a lot better song in French as "boule de gomme." Good enough to make him a superstar in Quebec and Europe.

Moe Berg

The founder of The Pursuit Of Happiness and the author of our #32 single, "I'm An Adult Now", Moe Berg grew up in Edmonton before joining the Queen Street. West scene in Toronto in the mid-eighties. Heavily influenced by Top Forty radio in the seventies, Moe has crafted a whole string of pop gems, including "She's So Young", "Hard To Laugh", and "Gretzky Rocks". Since TPOH has quieted down, Moe's been mostly producing up-and-coming Canadian acts and writing fiction. His collection of short stories is called *The Green Room*.

1. **CRAZY JANE –Tom Northcott**
Tom Northcott was a hippie folk singer I listened to as a kid. "Crazy Jane" is a brilliant song with a long, melancholy ending that a producer/record company would probably edit out if it were recorded today.

LIGHTHOUSE

2. **PRETTY LADY – Lighthouse**
This song was a huge influence on me as a songwriter. After hearing "Pretty Lady" on CHED-AM when I was sixteen, I ripped it off for the next two years.

3. **UNDERWHELMED – Sloan**
My entire Top 10 could easily be all Sloan tunes. They've recorded lots of amazing singles since, but this one is so unbearably clever it fully deserves Top 10 status.

4. **FROM THE BACK OF THE FILM – Thrush Hermit**
The best Canadian rock and roll song of all time. I've played this at my deejay gig at the Tap [in Toronto] every Saturday night for four years.

5. **SOUR SUITE – The Guess Who**
"Sour Suite" has been in my Top 10 since the day I first heard it. I'm still not sure what this is about, but Burton Cummings spoke to my teenage heart when he released this beautiful track.

6. **SOME SING, SOME DANCE – Pagliaro**
I can't think of a short quip that would adequately describe this masterpiece. Pagliaro is a national treasure.

7. **ANOTHER WAY OUT – Brave Belt**
Lyrically and musically, this sounded like what Randy Bachman did in The Guess Who. I guess it made sense for him to move on and explore the heavy music of BTO, but "Another Way Out" was, in my opinion, his greatest moment.

8. **DROP YOUR GUNS – April Wine**
Cowbell in the verse, three-part harmonies in the chorus, and twin guitars in the solo. This goblet of vintage Wine is rock and roll heaven.

9. **COYOTE – Joni Mitchell**
No Canadian artist has had a greater effect on me than Joni Mitchell. I'm more of a "deep tracks" Joni fan — her singles are so ubiquitous, it would be like picking "Satisfaction" by The Stones. However,

"Coyote", with its rich imagery and manic chord changes, is too good to leave off.

10. **THE REAL THING – Pointed Sticks**
These guys were on Quintessence and Stiff, the two coolest labels around when I was a kid, and recorded three classic pop singles. This was my favourite.

Honourable mentions:
DOLLAR IN MY POCKET – Big House;
HOT CHILD IN THE CITY – Nick Gilder;
DON'T DO NO GOOD TO CRY – The Poppy Family

85 Cuts Like A Knife

Bryan Adams

A&M, 1983

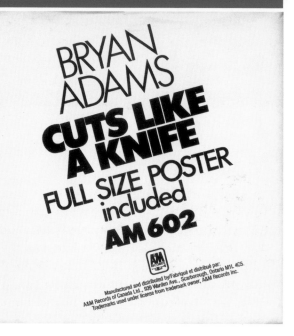

"A recording that signalled Adams was ready for the majors."

— Larry Leblanc, *The Leblanc Newsletter*

The title track from Adams's third album, this single, along with "Straight From The Heart" and "This Time", made him a star in North America. Our chat with the authors continues:

Bryan Adams: It was written in Jim's basement in West Vancouver, and it came out of a jam we had going. When we wrote back then, I used to sing and play guitar, Jim would play bass. I came up with the line "it cuts like a knife"; Jim responded with "but it feels so right" . . . pretty simple.

Jim Vallance: Songwriting is trial and error. Countless hours, fishing for ideas. The trick is knowing when you've got something good. Once we had that first bit of lyric, the rest of the song followed from there.

Bob Mersereau: Did you think you had something?

BA: Oh yes, it was a big, big moment for us. We knew we had written something special. I think I blew up my car speakers playing it so loud on the way home.

JV: We recorded a quick demo, just me, Bryan, and [band guitar player] Keith Scott. We knew we had a strong song, but you never know how things will turn out when it's released.

BM: It's a fine example of that classic lyric, "na-na-na-na-na-na-na-na." Did you run out of words, or did it feel so right?

BA: Yes, we intentionally ran out of words. I don't remember how the reprise got started, but it was undoubtedly something to do with us both loving "Hey Jude" by The Beatles.

JV: Typically, at the end of a song, you'd go back and repeat the chorus a few more times. But it felt like it needed something more, something a bit different.

BM: What was the feeling when the song broke?

BA: Oddly, it was as if it had always been there. Jim and I had our peak writing period between the years of 1983 and 1984. We were kind of unstoppable at that time.

JV: It shot all the way to number six on the Billboard Rock chart, which was a big deal back then, very exciting. This is the song that tipped the scales for us.

86 The Hockey Song

Stompin' Tom Connors

Boot, 1972

"I loved Stompin' Tom as a little timer, still do."

— Kirk Lahey, Universal Music

Just tell me this: when *Hockey Night In Canada* lost the rights to its famous theme song in 2008, why wasn't "The Hockey Song" immediately chosen as the successor? Every Canadian knows and loves it. Its lyrics speak to the grand tradition of gathering around the TV on Saturday night. It's the one event that holds this country together, old and young, families and friends, regardless of race, region, language, or gender. It is the best game you can name.

Hockey and popular music have formed a unique partnership in recent years. The game is as strong a part of Canadian culture as any of the arts, and many songwriters, diehard hockey fans, have celebrated hockey and its stars. The Pursuit Of Happiness scored with "Gretzky Rocks". The Tragically Hip brought back an almost forgotten Leafs hero of the 1950s, Bill Barilko, in "Fifty Mission Cap".

Canadian musicians don't only sing the praises, they also play the game. Each year at the Juno Awards, stars such as Jim Cuddy, George Canyon, and Sarah McLachlan lace up in support of MusiCounts, Canada's music education charity, in the Juno Cup. There's the difference between Canada and the United States: can you imagine Pink and Kanye West putting on football gear instead of posing on the red carpet? Rheostatics' Dave Bidini has forged an entire second career as a successful author, with books such as *Tropic Of Hockey* and *The Best Game You Can Name*, its title taken from Stompin' Tom's song.

Perhaps *Hockey Night In Canada* thought Stompin' Tom was out of touch with the young fans its advertisers need to court. This survey suggests otherwise. "The Hockey Song" has eclipsed long-time Connors favourites such as "Bud The Spud" and "Sudbury Saturday Night", especially among younger voters. Musically, it's as outdated as possible, a simple country-flavoured singalong, with a tune that's better suited to a summer camp than to modern airplay. But it's a combination of three great pillars of Canadian society: hockey, songwriting, and Stompin' Tom. You can't beat that lineup.

87 Wheat Kings

The Tragically Hip
MCA, 1992

"The instruments weave in and out, playing off each other, pushing and pulling, ebbing and flowing."

— Eden Munro, *Vue Weekly*

On The Tragically Hip's 1989 album *Up To Here*, the song "38 Years Old" tells the story of an escape from Millhaven Institution, the maximum security prison near Kingston, Ontario, the group's hometown. The song is fiction, but for one person it struck close to home.

David Milgaard had been wrongfully convicted of the murder of Gail Miller in Saskatchewan in 1969. He had always maintained his innocence, and his family had fought a long battle to get a new trial. In 1991, his appeal was finally being considered. According to Hip guitarist Rob Baker, speaking of the song in *The Top 100 Canadian Albums*, Milgaard had been in touch with the band regarding "38 Years Old", which sparked the group's interest in his story. Just a few months before the release of "Wheat Kings", Milgaard was a free man, as a stay of proceedings was ordered in his case. Later, DNA evidence proved his innocence, and another man was convicted of the murder.

Gord Downie's lyrics are often cryptic, built on images and influences only Downie can fully explain. He can be just as cryptic when questioned about them. "Wheat Kings" is usually described as partially about Milgaard, but in this case Downie wants to make his inspiration clear: "This song is entirely about David Milgaard and his faith in himself. And about his mother, Joyce, and her absolute faith in her son's innocence. And about our big country and its faith in man's fallibility. And about Gail Miller, all those mornings ago, just lying there, all her faith bleeding out into that Saskatoon snowbank."

Soon after his release, Milgaard met the band and got to hear the song in concert. It's become part of his story, and it's often the first time listeners hear about Milgaard and the problem of wrongful convictions. It's a bittersweet connection for Downie: "I was pleased, of course, and saddened. It's a sad story. It took too long."

88 Mon pays

Gilles Vigneault

Columbia, 1965

"Two minutes of unequivocal love for the soul and majesty of our land. If you aren't moved by it, you have no heart."

— Ralph Alfonso,
Bongo Beat Records

In two minutes and seven seconds, Gilles Vigneault summed up a nation. Really, he did it in the first line: "Mon pays, ce n'est pas un pays, c'est l'hiver" — My country is not a country, it's winter. It is often considered the unofficial national anthem of francophones in Quebec.

Vigneault didn't start out to compose a song that would achieve such iconic status. It was a cash job, similar to the story behind Gordon Lightfoot's creation of "Canadian Railroad Trilogy", another song often regarded as a wonderful reflection of the country. Vigneault was commissioned to write a song for the National Film Board's *La neige a fondu sur la Manicouagan*. Snow was the theme so Vigneault incorporated images of deepest winter, isolation, and storms. For Vigneault the poet, the weather became a metaphor: the culture of Quebec seen as isolated and distinct. There was brotherhood as well, the people connected through this wintry, spacious land.

"Mon pays" was immediately grabbed by many in Quebec who longed for a voice and a national identity. Its timing was perfect, coming as the Quiet Revolution blossomed. Its singalong quality and gorgeous melody led inspired crowds to break into song at every conceivable gathering, from political conventions to sporting events. Yet Vigneault denied he set out to compose a political or anthemic song. Certainly, he was reflecting the new thoughts of nationhood in the province, and he would often include social and political expressions in his writing. In the next decade, he worked at length for the cause of sovereignty.

Has the tune entered your head yet? It's one of the most memorable compositions in our musical heritage. Even if you aren't familiar with this famous French melody, you've probably heard it a thousand times on classic rock radio. It was borrowed wholesale for Patsy Gallant's huge 1976 disco hit, "From New York To L.A.", which went Top Ten in much of the world, though the new lyrics were slightly less poetic.

89 Home For A Rest

Spirit Of The West

Warner, 1990

"I have yet to be at a Canadian bar where people don't freak out when this is played."

— Chuck Teed, musician

"Home For A Rest" is one of the great bar songs, a singalong, lift-your-glass number that has found a huge life on Canadian campuses, a Frosh Week anthem. It feels like a party, and that's because it tells the tale of a really good one. Geoffrey Kelly remembers it well: "Recapping the whole story, it was just a bunch of misguided musicians trying to make a go of a poorly planned tour. It was more of an adventure than a tour. Looking back now, it was marvellous."

It stems from the early days of the Celtic band. Their Western Canadian take on traditional music was catching on, and the band members felt it was time to take in the Old Country. "Oh boy, it's entirely based in truth," reveals Kelly about the trip. "It tells the story of our first English tour, 1986. We barely had any gigs, and we were there for six weeks. We didn't know what we were doing, and it ended up being a big drinking fest. We just went, hoped for the best, and got away with it. We've all had those kinds of holidays where you push the envelope so much you need another holiday to recover."

Along with Great Big Sea and other East Coast acts, Spirit Of The West made Celtic music a hit in the country. "I was surprised the younger audience picked up on it," says Kelly. "Once we realized, yes, we can make this happen, we chased it. Up until then, folk festivals hadn't had a lot of that. All the traditional bands would sit down to play at workshops, and we'd be up on stage rocking and dancing.

"We played every university right across the country. Campuses got into us, and that's when we were at our peak, when we were straddling both audiences, a foot in the folk world and one on campus." Since then, every September, a new round of college freshmen all of a sudden discover they have Celtic roots, thanks to "Home For A Rest".

90 Letter From An Occupant

The New Pornographers

Mint, 2000

Carl Newman had been in an excellent 1990s Vancouver band, Zumpano, which drifted to a halt, and he found a new career. "I worked for a few years at this guitar company, which was a kind of crappy job," he says. "For the first year or two, I felt kind of happy because I'd always been this struggling musician, and finally I was just a guy with a regular paycheque, even if I wasn't making a massive amount. I thought, I can see why 90 per cent of the population lives like this. But then, like that 90 per cent, I got really sick of it, and thought, God, there's gotta be some other way out.

"I'd essentially given up on any sort of music career, but I knew I wanted to keep making music. So The New Pornographers was that project." He started recording in 1998, including "Letter From An Occupant", with Neko Case singing lead. "It's funny because it sat in the can for a couple of years," says Newman. "I remember being shocked because that one, and the three other songs we finished, I was really proud of. And then I was shocked because there was so little interest. I stopped thinking about it, and periodically friends would hear it and talk about how much they liked it."

In 2000, the Mint record label was putting together a compilation, and Newman offered them "Letter". Mint signed the band for a full album. Critics loved it, and the powerful vocals of Case were also a highlight. "That's the one thing I feel a certain amount of pride in," says Newman.

"I feel like I was a really amazing talent scout. I found Neko Case and Dan Behar, two people at the time nobody considered major talents, but now, twelve years later, people think of them as major talents."

"Raw excitement and musical joy . . . my favourite Canadian song of all time."

— Grant Lawrence, CBC Radio

Once again, Newman was out of the nine-to-five world: "It's all been kind of shocking, it's shocking to find myself working on our fifth album now. It's my job now, I'd be a fool to stop."

91 No Time

The Guess Who

RCA, 1969

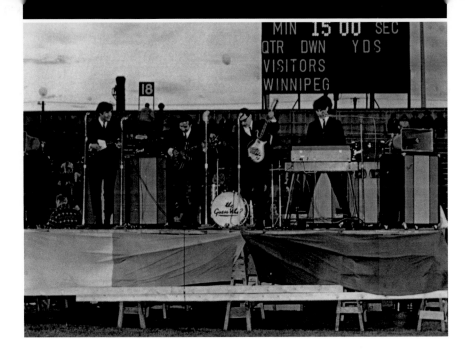

"Love Randy Bachman's guitar riff. Legendary."

— Andy Curran,
SRO Management

The Guess Who were finally enjoying hits by 1969, after working most of the decade to get there. The smash "These Eyes" and the double-sided hit "Laughing"/"Undun" had won over Canadian and US audiences. The only trouble was that all of these, despite being wonderful songs, were ballads, and the group members wanted to rock.

Randy Bachman knew they had to get something different out before audiences pigeonholed them: "Of course, we were dying to be the rock band we knew we were. It was actually a short transition period from 'These Eyes' to 'No Time.'"

That song had already been released on the album *Canned Wheat*, but there was a problem: it sounded like crap. Bachman: "We all agreed, and [producer] Jack Richardson thought 'No Time' had the potential of a hit song: guitar riffs, good melody, singalong chorus, harmonies.

"The first recording that was done at RCA Studios was very poor quality, but we knew the song was a great song. We thought we'd give 'No Time' another chance. Recording in the new RCA Studios in Chicago, we suddenly got 'our sound.' It began a new era of sonic recording coolness for The Guess Who."

As usual, Bachman brought his scholarly knowledge of the record charts to the composition. With its fuzz-tone guitar introduction, "No Time" leapt out of the car radio speaker. "I consciously make every song have a recognizable intro," he says. "I did study the best: Elvis, Chuck Berry, The Beatles. Every one of their hits, BAM! You know what it is before they even get to the chorus, which is what the title usually is, or where it's sung the first time."

It was the right move at the right time, as the Woodstock generation was looking for something heavier. "It brought us into the credible band zone because it was country rock," thinks Bachman. "It was the rage at that time with Buffalo Springfield, Poco, The Flying Burrito Brothers, Crosby, Stills & Nash. We were hip." Next would be "American Woman".

92 As The Years Go By

Mashmakhan
Columbia, 1970

"Cranked-up organ with the minor key melody and that energy you can only get from guys playing together in the same room at the same time."

— Jay Semko, musician

The musicians in Mashmakhan were veterans of the Montreal R&B scene when they put this new group together. The sound mirrored the progressive nature of the city, which was ahead of North America in welcoming elements of jazz and prog-rock style coming from Europe. Then there was the French accent in the vocals.

"We were fearless, man," laughs Rayburn Blake, the guitar player. "It was partly fearless, partly we just didn't give a crap what anybody thought, because we were having so much fun. When I met Pierre [Sénécal, singer-organist], he didn't speak any English, and my French was modest. He wrote 'As The Years Go By' when he had only been speaking English six or seven years. Some of it's a little unusual in its phrasing, but that's the French you're sensing. We left it alone, because we knew it was working."

People also loved the unique opening, a combination of Sénécal's organ and Blake's guitar hitting a one-note riff. It topped the Canadian charts and went Top Ten in the United States, but it was in Japan that it went through the roof.

"It was the second-biggest single Japan had seen up to that time," says Blake. "Only 'Bridge Over Troubled Water' was a bigger record. We played Tokyo for sixty-five thousand people, and we played Osaka for about forty thousand. We landed late at night, and there were about four thousand people at the airport waiting to greet us. There were a dozen little twelve-year-old girls with bouquets of flowers. I look out the window and they're actually rolling a red carpet out."

Back in Canada, Blake had his own epiphany about the scope of the hit. "I remember coming to Toronto, and I went to the CNE. It was just amazing, every ride in the place was playing 'As The Years Go By'. It's a great ride song. The Tilt-a-Whirl to 'As The Years Go By'."

93 Hey Hey, My My (Into The Black)/ My My, Hey Hey (Out Of The Blue)

Neil Young
Reprise, 1979

"Neil and Crazy Horse rocked the cuffs off my jeans when they launched into 'Hey Hey, My My'."

— Paul Templeman, CBC-TV

The crucial tracks of the *Rust Never Sleeps* album, these two songs start and finish the disc, with the "Out Of The Blue" version kicking off the acoustic side and "Into The Black" finishing off the electric flip side. They were first debuted a year before the album's release. The solo acoustic version came first, at a series of shows at The Boarding House in San Francisco called the "One Stop World Tour". Young rolled out several of the coming *Rust* tracks during the five-night, ten-show stand.

Four months later, he was ready to take the whole concept on the road. He called in Crazy Horse, which had been lying dormant since 1976. The *Rust Never Sleeps* tour was one of Young's biggest productions, complete with giant props, roadies dressed as *Star Wars* characters, and even some acting, as he woke up childlike on the stage. Both the acoustic and the electric versions of the song were in every show of the tour.

The song showcases the split typical of Young's work throughout his career: he's always been torn between the acoustic, solo performances, and the full-bore rock band. As with "Tonight's The Night" and "Rockin' In The Free World", we get both, one haunted, one heavy. Certainly the idea of the song is steeped in confusion. Young, having witnessed the birth of punk, can't decide if old rockers like himself, the Woodstock stars, have a future in the new music world. Is it better to fade away, as his career had been slowly doing in the 1970s, or burn out quickly, like Johnny Rotten did, quitting The Sex Pistols when the band hit the United States?

The electric side was the single version, a modest hit, but a career saver. Young was back in the public's esteem, and many critics named *Rust Never Sleeps* album of the year. With the parade of subpar albums he put out for many years after, at least he could point to the *Rust* concept as proof he wasn't a sixties relic.

Sass Jordan

Just when you thought you had Sass Jordan figured out, she succeeds at something else in her career. The Juno-winning belter has sold over a million discs and been named *Billboard* magazine's Best Female Rock Vocalist. She's a songwriter and an accomplished actress, working on stage and screen. And then there's that little extra job — as one of the judges on *Canadian Idol*, which has brought her a whole new kind of recognition. Now she puts her judging abilities to use for her personal Top 10 list. You'll notice a quite a few Quebec acts, reflecting her hometown of Montreal.

1. SAY HELLO – April Wine
Sheer catchiness, hook-laden, singalong, from the great Jerry Mercer's hypnotic drumbeat opening. Myles Goodwyn triumphs again — a fantastic songwriter.

2. CE SOIR ON DANSE AU NAZILAND – Nanette Workman
One of the greatest white female singers of all time, singing an iconic song from the awesome rock opera *Starmania*. Hard to beat.

3. CLOSER TOGETHER – The Box
Like most of the songs from this fantastic, underrated band, great lyric and glorious sound, from the bass voices to the counterpoint female voices, uplifting and happy!

4. KING OF THE HEAP – Odds
Another brilliant and underrated bunch of songwriters. Gorgeous song, moody and killer cool.

5. FALLEN ANGEL – Robbie Robertson
Searing and haunting, like so much of his work.

RON SEXSMITH

6. HANDS OF TIME – Ron Sexsmith
Melodically it just works for me. Beautifully crafted writing from one of Canada's most glorious songwriters.

7. POUR UN INSTANT – Harmonium
One of the great Quebec bands that put French music into another league. Introspective and intimate at the same time as it seeps across a wide and meandering soundscape.

8. LES BOMBES – Michel Pagliaro
An incredible, dark, brooding, scary, prophetic GENIUS of a song and songwriter.

9. ANIMALS – Nickelback
Perfect anthemic cock-rock at its punch-you-in-the-face, hooky-stupid-but-real-lyrics best! Arena rock, perfectly executed.

10. ISABELLE – Jean Leloup
A wicked ska bust-up from the unknown genius Jean Leloup, now known as Jean Leclerc.

94 Diana

Paul Anka

Sparton, 1957

"Rock and roll was pretty much the domain of the Americans back in the early days. Ottawa's Paul Anka proved to the world, and more importantly to Canadians, that we could do it, too."

— Lee Marshall, broadcaster

Ottawa's Anka has had a career unparalleled in show business. Songwriter, performer, actor, and hitmaker, he's moved from the early rock and roll era to the glitz of Vegas showrooms to writing one of the most famous TV themes of all time to helping create the last new song of Michael Jackson's career.

He's written dozens of classics for himself and others, including Buddy Holly's "It Doesn't Matter Anymore", "She's A Lady" for Tom Jones, and "My Way" for Frank Sinatra. When Johnny Carson took over as host of *The Tonight Show*, Anka came up with the theme music, and he co-wrote "This Is It" with the King of Pop.

His first tour was with The Everly Brothers, Chuck Berry, and The Drifters. He was on the "Winter Dance Party" tour in 1959 that saw Holly, The Big Bopper, and Richie Valens perish. In 2005, he made an acclaimed album called *Rock Swings*, doing Big Band versions of songs by Oasis, Soundgarden, and R.E.M. He discovered John Prine, and helped Corey Hart and Michael Bublé get started. To launch his own career, he simply wrote and performed the biggest-selling single of the rock and roll era up to that time, a staggering ten million copies. When he was sixteen.

Written about an older girl he knew in high school, "Diana" is a classic bit of unrequited love, with a touch of doo-wop and a big helping of showbiz. The song, and his youth, made Anka a natural for TV, and he became a regular on *Ed Sullivan* and other big broadcasts, where he was seen as much less dangerous and controversial than Elvis or Jerry Lee Lewis. Throughout his whole career, Anka has always found a way to stay at the top of the charts, or on the biggest shows, or behind the best-selling hits. He's money in the bank.

95 The Maker

Daniel Lanois

Opal, 1989

One of the world's busiest producers, for such as Bob Dylan, U2, and Emmylou Harris, Lanois also finds time for his own recording and performing career. Here, he checks in with these exclusive thoughts on his best-loved song:

"Images of the River Liffey in Dublin, Ireland, every night walking home, the river almost spilling its black ink water into the dockland warehouse area of Dublin. My home was the Gresham Hotel. I was working with U2 on their *The Unforgettable Fire* record. My journey home took me by the two Guinness ships, often docked by the studio on the Liffey, having their bellies filled, readying for the Guinness transport to England. Guinness beer was still being shipped to Liverpool twice a week in

1984. The black calmness of the river at night made it look like a mirror. On a moonlit night, I could see my reflection in the river, and when I listened the river spoke to me.

"Oh deep water, black and cold like the night, I stand with arms wide open. I've run a twisted line, I'm a stranger in the eyes of the Maker. I could not see for the fog in my eyes, I could not feel for the fear in my life, from across the great divide, in the distance I saw a light, Jean-Baptiste walking to me with the Maker. My body is bent and broken by long and danger sleep, I can't work the fields

of Abraham and turn my head away, I'm not a stranger in the hands of the Maker. Brother John, have you seen the homeless daughter standing there with broken wings? I have seen the flaming sword there, over there east of Eden, burning in the eyes of the Maker. Oh river, rise from your sleep, river rise from your sleep, rise from your sleep.

"The lyrics to 'The Maker' had come up from the river. The music to 'The Maker' came out of New Orleans. This personal spiritual song was about to become more public with a Willie Nelson rendition."

"I'm thankful for Daniel Lanois. He's inspiring. The song is so beautifully written, so is the music, very soothing."
— Meghan Scott, Tuck and Roll Productions

96 Nova Heart

Spoons
Ready, 1982

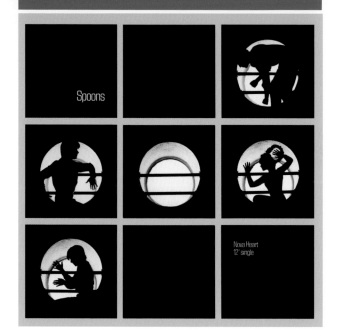

Spoons

Nova Heart
12" single

"Defines New Romantic music for me and the eighties pretty much. I haven't quite figured out the lyrics yet or what they mean but it's perfection nonetheless."

— David Gawdunyk, Megatunes

Spoons came together at Aldershot High School in Burlington, Ontario, when Gordon Deppe met Sandy Horne. "Sandy and I came out of the high school band," says Deppe. "I kinda liked her, I thought she was cute. We were on a school trip, and we pulled out a couple of acoustic guitars. I think it was just because we were friends, and she was a prospective girlfriend at the time."

Originally a progressive rock band, Spoons managed to be on the forefront of new sounds that were changing music. "When the New Wave thing came in in the early eighties, there was so much variety in electronica and drama," says Deppe. "I said, wait a second, maybe we could get a shot at this, maybe we could slip in there because we were quirky. Just by making a few little changes, it strangely fits. So that's how it began, a nerdy progressive band that jumped on the New Wave bandwagon."

It all came together with "Nova Heart". Spoons were one of the first Canadian groups to use a hand-clap drum machine beat, one of the first to get championed on the new, important college radio circuit, and one of the first with a video for MuchMusic to play, "which was, of course, horrible, but at the time won lots of awards," Deppe snickers.

Nineteen-eighties music often gets derided for its synthesizers and bad haircuts, but Deppe says attitudes have changed: "There was a time in the nineties when we dropped out of the picture. It was a bad time for bands like us, and I never thought it would come around again. I think it was around '95, we did a tour for a Best-Of album, and it was better than some of the full-fledged tours we'd done back in the eighties. It's not embarrassing to be from the eighties anymore. Every year I think it's going to die out again, but it doesn't. People like that time, and they hold onto it."

97 La complainte du phoque en alaska

Beau Dommage

Capitol, 1974

"The ultimate sad waltz, the greatest love song ever written for mammals."

— Sylvain Cormier, *Le Devoir*

The poor seal. His love has left the ice floe in Alaska to make her living in the circus in the United States. It would make you sit on the ice and cry, too. It's not exactly the typical story for the pop charts, but Montreal's Beau Dommage turned the tale into a smash, one of the biggest-selling and most beloved hits of the era.

Along with Harmonium, Beau Dommage were the rulers of 1970s Quebec rock. Yet rock was never as strictly defined in Quebec as it was in the rest of the country. In Montreal's musical melting pot, anything could go into the mix. Beau Dommage borrowed liberally from folk and country, with a hint of progressive rock and the distinctive humour of Quebec's music.

"La complainte du phoque en Alaska" is quite soft, with a lovely lilt and an old-fashioned folk touch. By the second verse, a synthesizer sneaks in, and it becomes obvious this is a youth movement. It fit in nicely with the hippie vibe that was still around. The instrumental break later on shifts the song to a carnival waltz, with an imitation calliope, all done in a dreamy and gentle manner. Sweet harmonies make it a pleasure from start to finish.

It was such a smashing debut, and Beau Dommage quickly became record setters. The self-titled debut album went gold (50,000 in sales) in just a couple of weeks and eventually surpassed the triple platinum number of 300,000, making it not just a hit in Quebec, but matching the biggest sales numbers of any English-Canadian groups. Such was the group's popularity that their second album, 1975's *Où est passée la noce?* became the first in Canada to reach platinum status (sales of 100,000) on the day of release.

In a major tribute to a modern composition, iconic Quebec *chansonnier* Félix Leclerc recorded a version of the song. Its writer, group member Michel Rivard, started on a long and successful solo career even before Beau Dommage's 1978 break-up, becoming one of the biggest male stars in the province.

98 *Secret Heart*

Ron Sexsmith

Interscope, 1995

"It touches on a great and poignant territory not overmined in a universe of love songs."

— Sean Ashby, musician

Ron Sexsmith's 1995 eponymous CD quickly became the buzz of sharp-eared music fans after Elvis Costello championed it on the cover of the British music magazine *Uncut*. The song that leapt out was "Secret Heart", and signalled a return to singer-songwriter values. The alternative world grabbed onto simplicity again with artists who would include Jeff Buckley, Rufus Wainwright, Elliott Smith, and Ryan Adams.

"The eighties were a hard time to be a songwriter," recalls Sexsmith. "I couldn't get signed in the eighties. It changed with Nirvana. They were the bomb that came along and blew up the eighties. They weren't about all the hair and the makeup. All of a sudden, it was possible for someone like me to come along and sing songs that weren't ironic, that were straight-ahead. So I was really lucky that I got in the door when I did."

Famously covered by everyone from Rod Stewart to Feist to Diana Krall, it was nearly abandoned. "It's funny, my publisher didn't think that the song should even be on the record. He didn't think it was very strong. Mitchell [Froom, producer] felt it was the one I should open with, because he felt it was my calling card, I guess."

Sexsmith also considers it the turning point for his songwriting: "I'd been going to all the open stages [in Toronto], and I was hearing all these really great songwriters like Kyp Harness and Bob Snider who I just thought were incredible. They had these songs with multiple verses like Dylan does, or Leonard Cohen. I used to try to do that, but I wasn't very good at it. It forced me to go a whole other way and get more direct and write lyrics that were more simple. 'Secret Heart' was the first one, really, the first attempt. I was trying to write something that Buddy Holly might do, like 'True Love Ways'. So I was pretty happy with it. It did open the floodgates."

99 Run To You

Bryan Adams

A&M, 1984

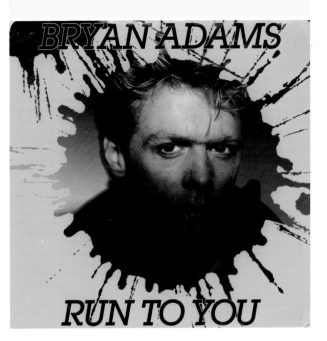

"The perfect mix of bombast three-chord rock with pop sensibilities. The song brought Canada into the eighties rock decade."

— Mitch Lafon, *BW & BK*

After the success of 1983's *Cuts Like A Knife* album, the songwriting team of Bryan Adams and Jim Vallance felt unstoppable. And the highs of 1983 were about to be eclipsed by the even-greater success of the *Reckless* album. The first hit off that album was "Run To You", which, as its authors explain, was almost given away.

Bob Mersereau: This was a bit darker, a song that sneaks up on you and hits you with the chorus. Was the idea to find something somewhere between ballad and rocker?

Bryan Adams: This was never written as a ballad. Funnily, we wrote this song with the intention to give it to Blue Oyster Cult, because they were being produced by our friend Bruce

Fairbairn. At that time, Bruce was always cutting our songs with the groups he was working with, bless his heart. BOC didn't like the song for one reason or another, so I ended up cutting it a year later for my *Reckless* album, thanks to [producer] Bob Clearmountain asking me for "one more song for the album."

Jim Vallance: We figured, if we can come up with a solid riff like "Reaper", then Blue Oyster Cult would love our song. As it turns out, they didn't! So Bryan recorded it himself, in one take. It was a last-minute addition to Bryan's album, almost an afterthought.

BM: Were you guys now aiming worldwide, and did that put

more pressure on the songwriting sessions?

BA: I don't think Jim and I ever acknowledged the forty-ninth parallel. It could be because we just wanted to make music we liked, so the bar was high. After *Reckless,* we were no longer struggling musicians. We had sold ten million albums and it was going strong. It was at that point that the internal pressure kicked in to follow up what we had done. It took us two albums to do it again with *Waking Up The Neighbours,* but we did it.

JV: By 1983, '84, we'd figured out how to write songs. From that point on, we just wanted to get better at it.

100 Weighty Ghost

Wintersleep

Labwork, 2007

"One of those songs that had me within the opening chords immediately. Still a song that is stuck in my head well after hearing it."

— Dale Robertson, Universal Music

Halifax band Wintersleep's breakthrough single was in jeopardy of being forgotten even before it was finished, because singer–guitar player Paul Murphy had to stop writing right in the middle of it. The person who almost wrecked their landmark tune was none other than Murphy's mother.

"It was after we were finished touring," says Murphy, "and I was going to drive to Yarmouth [Nova Scotia, his hometown] with my mom and younger brother. I started writing it in Halifax, the melody for the chorus. I remember calling Loel [Campbell, drummer] and asking him if he liked it. Then my mom wanted

to leave, so I had to remember the whole thing over the drive, having to have a conversation with mom and my brother, trying not to forget the melody. Then I finished it up in Yarmouth."

As we end our list of the Top 100 Canadian Singles with the most recent hit, it's a good time to point out the continuing importance of the single. While Wintersleep were a growing band, they were still relatively unknown before 2007. Murphy says the song made a huge difference: "It was the first time we'd had anything on the radio, or interest from those kinds of music listeners.

It was a whole new world for us. We were invited to play live on big radio stations, and doing interviews, we did get a boost. In Vancouver, the first time we played the Commodore it was insane. We'd gone quickly from two hundred, three hundred people to selling out six-thousand-people venues."

Although Murphy didn't grow up in a singles culture, he likes them a lot now. "It definitely did not bother me to have 'Weighty Ghost' as a single. We felt lucky to have that on the radio and to have people like it and play it. I like the idea of a single being a piece off a record that makes people want to buy the record."

That is what a hit single was, is, and continues to be: your new favourite song, by your new favourite band.

TOP 100 HIT PARADE
THE TOP 100 CANADIAN SINGLES

1.	AMERICAN WOMAN/ NO SUGAR TONIGHT	The Guess Who	RCA, 1970
2.	HEART OF GOLD	Neil Young	Reprise, 1972
3.	THE WEIGHT	The Band	Captiol, 1968
4.	SUMMER OF '69	Bryan Adams	A&M, 1985
5.	HALLELUJAH	Leonard Cohen	Columbia, 1984
6.	BORN TO BE WILD	Steppenwolf	Dunhil, 1968
7.	IF YOU COULD READ MY MIND	Gordon Lightfoot	Reprise, 1970
8.	TAKIN' CARE OF BUSINESS	Bachman-Turner Overdrive	Mercury, 1974
9.	FOUR STRONG WINDS	Ian & Sylvia	Vanguard, 1963
10.	SNOWBIRD	Anne Murray	Capitol, 1970

11.	BIG YELLOW TAXI	JONI MITCHELL	REPRISE, 1970
12.	TOM SAWYER	RUSH	MERCURY, 1981
13.	TRY	BLUE RODEO	RISQUE DISQUE, 1987
14.	NEW ORLEANS IS SINKING	THE TRAGICALLY HIP	MCA, 1989
15.	THE WRECK OF THE EDMUND FITZGERALD	GORDON LIGHTFOOT	REPRISE, 1976
16.	SUZANNE	LEONARD COHEN	COLUMBIA, 1967
17.	LIFE IS A HIGHWAY	TOM COCHRANE	CAPTIOL, 1991
18.	THESE EYES	THE GUESS WHO	NIMBUS 9, 1969
19.	SUNDOWN	GORDON LIGHTFOOT	REPRISE, 1974
20.	UNDERWHELMED	SLOAN	MURDERECORDS, 1992
21.	UP ON CRIPPLE CREEK/THE NIGHT THEY DROVE OLD DIXIE DOWN	THE BAND	CAPITOL, 1969
22.	LET YOUR BACKBONE SLIDE	MAESTRO FRESH-WES	ATTIC, 1989
23.	TIRED OF WAKING UP TIRED	THE DIODES	CBS, 1978
24.	THE SPIRIT OF RADIO	RUSH	MERCURY, 1980
25.	OH WHAT A FEELING	CROWBAR	DAFFODIL, 1971
26.	HIGH SCHOOL CONFIDENTIAL	ROUGH TRADE	TRUE NORTH, 1981
27.	ECHO BEACH	MARTHA AND THE MUFFINS	DINDISC, 1979
28.	SWEET CITY WOMAN	THE STAMPEDERS	MWC, 1971
29.	WAKE UP	ARCADE FIRE	MERGE, 2004
30.	IF I HAD $1000000	BARENAKED LADIES	INDEPENDENT, 1991
31.	LINDBERG	ROBERT CHARLEBOIS AVEC LOUISE FORESTIER	GAMMA, 1968
32.	I'M AN ADULT NOW	THE PURSUIT OF HAPPINESS	TPOH, 1986
33.	NOTHIN'	THE UGLY DUCKLINGS	YORKTOWN, 1966
34.	COAX ME	SLOAN	GEFFEN, 1994
35.	CLOSER TO THE HEART	RUSH	ANTHEM, 1977
36.	PICTURE MY FACE	TEENAGE HEAD	IGM, 1978
37.	SHAKIN' ALL OVER	THE GUESS WHO	QUALITY, 1965
38.	SIGNS	FIVE MAN ELECTRICAL BAND	LIONEL, 1971
39.	LOST TOGETHER	BLUE RODEO	WARNER, 1992
40.	SONNY'S DREAM	RON HYNES	GRAND EAST, 1981
41.	THE SAFETY DANCE	MEN WITHOUT HATS	STATIK, 1982
42.	CLAIRE	RHEOSTATICS	SIRE, 1994
43.	ONE FINE MORNING	LIGHTHOUSE	GRT, 1970
44.	(MAKE ME DO) ANYTHING YOU WANT	A FOOT IN COLDWATER	DAFFODIL, 1972
45.	SUNGLASSES AT NIGHT	COREY HART	AQUARIUS, 1983
46.	WORKING FOR THE WEEKEND	LOVERBOY	CBS, 1981
47.	RAISE A LITTLE HELL	TROOPER	MCA, 1978
48.	RISE UP	PARACHUTE CLUB	CURRENT/RCA 1983
49.	BLACK VELVET	ALANNAH MYLES	ATLANTIC, 1989
50.	SEASONS IN THE SUN	TERRY JACKS	GOLDFISH, 1974

51.	MONTRÉAL -40°	MALAJUBE	DARE TO CARE, 2006
52.	CINNAMON GIRL	NEIL YOUNG	REPRISE, 1969
53.	YOU OUGHTA KNOW	ALANIS MORISSETTE	MAVERICK, 1995
54.	1234	FEIST	ARTS & CRAFTS, 2007
55.	REBELLION (LIES)	ARCADE FIRE	MERGE, 2004
56.	CONSTANT CRAVING	K.D. LANG	SIRE, 1992
57.	ROCKIN' IN THE FREE WORLD	NEIL YOUNG	REPRISE, 1989
58.	LOVIN' YOU AIN'T EASY	PAGLIARO	MUCH, 1971
59.	LOVERS IN A DANGEROUS TIME	BRUCE COCKBURN	TRUE NORTH, 1984
60.	BOBCAYGEON	THE TRAGICALLY HIP	UNIVERSAL, 1998
61.	A CASE OF YOU/CALIFORNIA	JONI MITCHELL	REPRISE, 1971
62.	NEW YORK CITY	THE DEMICS	READY, 1979
63.	(EVERYTHING I DO) I DO IT FOR YOU	BRYAN ADAMS	A&M, 1991
64.	AHEAD BY A CENTURY	THE TRAGICALLY HIP	MCA, 1996
65.	5 DAYS IN MAY	BLUE RODEO	WARNER, 1993
66.	I'M MOVIN' ON	HANK SNOW	RCA, 1950
67.	POUR UN INSTANT	HARMONIUM	POLYGRAM, 1974
68.	MAGIC CARPET RIDE	STEPPENWOLF	ABC-DUNHILL, 1968
69.	MONEY CITY MANIACS	SLOAN	MURDERECORDS, 1998
70.	MY HEART WILL GO ON	CÉLINE DION	COLUMBIA, 1997
71.	CRABBUCKIT	K-OS	ASTRALWERKS, 2004
72.	THIS BEAT GOES ON/ SWITCHIN' TO GLIDE	THE KINGS	ELEKTRA, 1980
73.	OLD MAN/THE NEEDLE AND THE DAMAGE DONE	NEIL YOUNG	REPRISE, 1972
74.	1990	JEAN LELOUP	AUDIOGRAM, 1991
75.	EYES OF A STRANGER	PAYOLA$	A&M, 1982
76.	HASN'T HIT ME YET	BLUE RODEO	WARNER, 1993
77.	YOU AIN'T SEEN NOTHIN' YET	BACHMAN-TURNER OVERDRIVE	MERCURY, 1974
78.	WONDERING WHERE THE LIONS ARE	BRUCE COCKBURN	TRUE NORTH, 1979
79.	YOU COULD HAVE BEEN A LADY	APRIL WINE	AQUARIUS, 1972
80.	SOMETHING ON MY MIND/ LET'S SHAKE	TEENAGE HEAD	ATTIC, 1980
81.	HELP ME	JONI MITCHELL	ASYLUM, 1974
82.	WE'RE HERE FOR A GOOD TIME (NOT A LONG TIME)	TROOPER	MCA, 1977
83.	SUNNY DAYS	LIGHTHOUSE	GRT, 1972
84.	LE PETIT ROI	JEAN-PIERRE FERLAND	BARCLAY, 1970
85.	CUTS LIKE A KNIFE	BRYAN ADAMS	A&M, 1983
86.	THE HOCKEY SONG	STOMPIN' TOM CONNORS	BOOT, 1972
87.	WHEAT KINGS	THE TRAGICALLY HIP	MCA, 1992
88.	MON PAYS	GILLES VIGNEAULT	COLUMBIA, 1965
89.	HOME FOR A REST	SPIRIT OF THE WEST	WARNER, 1990
90.	LETTER FROM AN OCCUPANT	THE NEW PORNOGRAPHERS	MINT, 2000
91.	NO TIME	THE GUESS WHO	RCA, 1969
92.	AS THE YEARS GO BY	MASHMAKHAN	COLUMBIA, 1970
93.	HEY HEY, MY MY (INTO THE BLACK)/ MY MY, HEY HEY (OUT OF THE BLUE)	NEIL YOUNG	REPRISE, 1979
94.	DIANA	PAUL ANKA	SPARTON, 1957
95.	THE MAKER	DANIEL LANOIS	OPAL, 1989
96.	NOVA HEART	SPOONS	READY, 1982
97.	LA COMPLAINTE DU PHOQUE EN ALASKA	BEAU DOMMAGE	CAPTIOL, 1974
98.	SECRET HEART	RON SEXSMITH	INTERSCOPE, 1995
99.	RUN TO YOU	BRYAN ADAMS	A&M, 1984
100.	WEIGHTY GHOST	WINTERSLEEP	LABWORK, 2007

The Jurors

Bryan Acker, Herohill Blog, Halifax

Julie Adam, program director, CHFI, Toronto

Trevor Adams, *Halifax Magazine*, Halifax

Jelena Adzic, CBC-TV, Toronto

Scott Alan, 99.3 The Fox, Vancouver

Jean Alary, Warner Music, Montreal

Ralph Alfonso, Bongo Beat Records, Montreal

Brian Allen, AMPLUS Productions, Mississauga

Eric Alper, E1 Distribution, Toronto

Peter Anawati, CBC Radio, Fredericton

Cleave Anderson, musician, Hamilton

Jonathan Anderson, music maker, Langley, BC

Duane Andrews, musician, St. John's

Frank Andrews, CITI-FM, Winnipeg

Sean Ashby, musician, Toronto

Trinette Atkinson, KICX 91.7, Sudbury

Marina Atwell, Velocity Entertainment, Halifax

Guillaume Audy, Warner Music, Montreal

Ray Auffrey, Spin-It Records, Moncton

Alan Auld, Rock 94, Thunder Bay

Ryan Awram, CKKQ, Victoria

Shaun Bailey, music fan, Toronto

Joey Balducchi, musician, Blind Mule, Hamilton

Jill Barber, musician, Vancouver

Matthew Barber, musician, Toronto

Michael Barclay, blogger, Toronto

Brian Bartlett, poet, Halifax

Mark Bartlett, New York Society Library, New York City

Jeff Bateman, writer/editor, Sooke, BC

Scott Beadle, music fan, Vancouver

Ken Beattie, Publicity, Vancouver

Mia Beaulieu, music fan, Montreal

Anthony Bédard, music fan, Hull, QC

Tom Bedell, Q104, Halifax

Jaymz Bee, JAZZ FM, Toronto

Roxanne Bégin, Bonsound, Montreal

Adrien Begrand, music writer, Saskatoon

Antoine Bélanger, music fan, Montreal

Gabrielle Bélanger, music fan, Montreal

Mike Bell, Sonic Unyon Distribution, Hamilton

Greg Bennett, filmmaker, Toronto

Kent Bennett, musician, Toronto

Robert Benson, Bravo!, Toronto

Rosalie Bergeron, music fan, Montreal

Mikey Rishwain Bernard, M pour Montréal Festival, Montreal

Geoff Berner, musician, Vancouver

Édouard Bernier, music fan, Montreal

Don Berns, former broadcaster, Toronto

Dave Bidini, musician, Toronto

John Biggs, CHAM, Hamilton

Kim Bingham, artist/music producer, Montreal

Eli Bisonnette, Dare To Care Records, Montreal

Paul Bisson, CBC-TV, Ottawa

Fiona Black, Capilano College Arts Theatre, North Vancouver

Theresa Blackwell, Universal Music, Vancouver

Matt Blenkarn, music fan, Ottawa

Karen Bliss, music journalist, Toronto

Tom Blizzard, Radio Atlantic, Fredericton

Dean Blundell, 102.1 The Edge, Toronto

Caroline Bognar, Greenland Productions, Montreal

Steve Bolton, media professor, Loyalist College, Belleville, ON

William Bouchard, music fan, Montreal

Rose Boucher, music fan, Montreal

Janesta Boudreau, Sonic Entertainment Group, Halifax

Jonathan Boudreau, CD Plus (R.I.P.), Halifax

Andre Bourgeois, Instinct Artist Management, Halifax

Monique Bourque, Radio-Canada, Moncton

Adam Bowie, *The Daily Gleaner*, Fredericton

Rob Bowman, York University, Toronto

Lionel Boxer, music consumer, Melbourne, Australia

Sam Boyd, BMF Productions, Brampton, ON
Paul Boynett, Bravo!, Toronto
Edgar Breau, musician, Hamilton
Robin Brock, musician, Vancouver
Dan Brooks, Key Music Group, Hamilton
Russell Broom, musician/producer, Calgary
Pierre Brousseau, CFID, Acton Vale, QC
Keith Brown, Aquarius Records, Montreal
Marion Brunelle, Live Jazz, Montreal
Bob Bryden, musician, Burlington
Adam Bunch, *SoundProof Magazine*, Toronto
Michael Burke, Cordova Bay, Victoria
Peter Burnside, Pacemaker Entertainment, Toronto
Lauren Burrows, CBC Radio 3, Vancouver
Gary Cable, music lawyer, Sherwood Park, AB
Leonardo Calcagno, Amnesia Marketing, Montreal
Deane Cameron, EMI Music, Toronto
Ron Camilleri, music producer/writer, Mississauga
Mike Campbell, manager, Halifax
Tommy Campbell, author/actor, London, UK
Darrin Cappe, Tempus Fugit, Toronto
Jean-François Cardin, Iguana Management, Montreal
Elizabeth Caron, music fan, Montreal
Cam Carpenter, manager, Toronto
Lorraine Carpenter, *Montreal Mirror*, Montreal
Philip Carr, music fan, Calgary
Joel Carriere, Bedlam Music, Toronto
Cub Carson, Virgin Radio, Ottawa
Rebecca Case, manager, Toronto
Cassandra Caverhill, CJAM, Windsor
Michel Cécyre, Radio-Canada, Montreal
Rod Chabot, HMV, Quebec City
Adrian Chamberlain, *Victoria Times*, Victoria
Sébastien Charest, Montreal International Music Initiative, Montreal
Matt Charlton, Pigeon Row Public Relations, Halifax
Scott Chasty, Rock 94, Thunder Bay
Brian Chick, Universal Music, Toronto
André Chouinard, Radio-Canada, Quebec City

Marc Chouinard, Capitol Theatre, Moncton
Jenna Chow, CBC Radio, Vancouver
Jarrett Churchill, Metro Canada, Toronto
Stephen Clare, music writer, Halifax
Darin Clark, Z99, Red Deer
David Clarke, Grooves Records, London
Jennifer Claveau, musician, Toronto
Léa Cloutier, music fan, Montreal
Steve Coady, Warner Music, Toronto
Meg Coffie, music fan, Ottawa
Eric Cohen, MSN/Sympatico Music Channel, Toronto
April Coish, Jane Harbury Publicity, Toronto
Leah Collins, Dose.ca, Toronto
Steve Colwill, CHEZ 106, Ottawa
Carl Comeau, Hyperbole Music Management, Montreal
Robin Connelly, CJKL-FM, Kirkland Lake, ON
Shawn Conner, writer/publisher, Vancouver
Andrew Connors, filmmaker, Whitehorse
Ben Conoley, Punknews.org, Fredericton
J.D. Considine, *The Globe and Mail*, Toronto
Jose Contreras, musician, Montreal
Stephen Cooke, *The Chronicle Herald*, Halifax
Tom Cooke, Standard Radio, Hamilton
Judith Coombe, Starfish Entertainment, Toronto
John Corcelli, CBC Radio, Toronto
Brian Corless, music collector, Dartmouth
Sylvain Cormier, *Le Devoir*, Montreal
Michel Corriveau, Radio-Canada, Fredericton
Warren Cosford, producer/programmer, Windsor
Anne Côté, Radio Énergie, Quebec City
Samuel Côté, music fan, Montreal
Véronique Côté, présidente, RSVP Media, Montreal
Doug Cox, musician/producer, Vancouver Island
Murray Crawford, Trent University, Peterborough, ON

Jim Cressman, Cressman Sakamoto Agency, Calgary
Marc Crevier, Universal Music, Winnipeg
Colin Cripps, musician, Hamilton
Steven Croatto, Énergie 98.9, Quebec City
Caitlin Crockard, CBC Radio, Ottawa
Alan Cross, host, *Ongoing History of New Music* and ExploreMusic.com, Toronto
Krista Culp, FACTOR, Toronto
Andy Curran, SRO Management, Toronto
Jen Cymek, Listen Harder Publicity, Toronto
Lori D'Agostino, S.L. Feldman & Associates, Toronto
Gerald Da Sylva, Proxima Marketing, Laval, QC
Dolores Dagenais, musician, Pictou, NS
Fran Dalziel, music fan, Hamilton
Josh Darrell, music fan, Saint John
Noémie Darveau, CISM-FM, Montreal
Penny Davidson, music fan, Toronto
Frank Davies, record producer/music publisher, Toronto
John Davies, Sony Music, Toronto
Phil Dellio, CKLN-FM, Toronto
Sari Delmar, Audio Blood Media, Toronto
Mitch DePalma, Warner Music, Montreal
Stuart Derdeyn, *The Province*, Vancouver
Dave DeRocco, Y108, Hamilton
Mathieu Desjardins, music fan, Montreal
Sonia Dickin, musician, Saskatoon
Denis Dion, compositeur, Trois-Rivières
Guy Dixon, *The Globe and Mail*, Toronto
Moe Doiron, *The Globe and Mail*, Toronto
Carla Donnell, Magic 106.1, Guelph
Luke Doucet, musician, Hamilton
J.C. Douglas, Newcap Broadcasting, Halifax
Raina Douris (Edge Girl), The Edge, Toronto
Lloyd Doyle, manager, Charlottetown
Lyle Drake, Avondale Music, St. John's
Stéphane Drolet, Sony Music, Montreal
Chris Drossos, Universal Music, Toronto
Howard Druckman, SOCAN, Toronto
Victor Dubé, music fan, Quebec City
Matt Duboff, Brandon Folk, Music & Art Festival, Brandon
Christopher Duda, journalist, Toronto

Darren Dumas, musician, Toronto
Étienne Dumont, 104.5 CKOY, Sherbrooke
Curtis Dunat, Magic 106, Guelph
Andrea Dunn, CFPL, London
Malissa Dunphy, X92.9, Calgary
James Duplacey, historian/author, Calgary
Carola Duran, M pour Montréal Festival, Montreal
Sophie Durocher, *Le Journal de Montréal*, Montreal
John Einarson, music writer, Winnipeg
Corrie Eisenberg, Iceberg 85, Toronto
Michael Elves, UMFM, Winnipeg
Danielle Emmrich, Starfish Entertainment, Toronto
Russ Empey, CJAY 92, Calgary
Andrea England, musician, Toronto
Anne Robin Ettles, musician, Pointe-du-Chêne, NB
Yann Falquet, musician, Genticorum, Montreal
Rob Farina, CHUM, Toronto
Brian Farquharson, Anya Wilson Publicity, Toronto
Johnston Farrow, music writer, Halifax
Simon Fauteux, SIX Media Marketing, Montreal
Elizabeth Fawcett, music fan, Toronto
Enzo Fazari, musician, Richmond Hill
Bonnie Fedrau, SoStarStruck, Toronto
Cori Ferguson, Cori Ferguson Publicity, Toronto
Will Ferguson, author, Calgary
Bernie Finkelstein, Finkelstein Management Company, Toronto
Roy "Bim" Forbes, musician, North Vancouver
Maelie Fortin, music fan, Montreal
Norm Foster, actor/playwright, Toronto
Stephen Foster, musician, Hamilton
Julien Fournier, music fan, Montreal
Kathryn Fox, writer, Halifax
Diane Foy, Skylar Entertainment, Toronto
Wayne Francis, musician, Charlottetown
Laura Fraser, Stage Door Promotion & Publicity, Toronto
Dave Freeman, Club Bass, Toronto

Sarah French, Sarah French Publicity, Toronto
Andy Frost, Q107, Toronto
Chris Fudge, music fan, Saint John
Mako Funasaka, Talkin' Blues Media, Toronto
Émile Gagné, music fan, Montreal
Félix Gagnon, music fan, Montreal
Juliette Gagnon, music fan, Montreal
Doug Gallant, *The Guardian*, Charlottetown
Meghan Gamble, Open Road Recordings, Toronto
François Gariépy, Astral Media, Québec City
Bill Garrett, Borealis Records, Toronto
Mark Gaudet, musician, Moncton
Jean-Paul Gauthier, Hamilton Music Awards, Hamilton
Thomas Gauthier, music fan, Quebec City
David Gawdunyk, Megatunes, Edmonton
Lana Gay, CBC Radio 3, Vancouver
Randy Gelling, CFUV, Victoria
Sam Giancanada, music fan, Vancouver
Ron Gillespie, Ocean 100, Charlottetown
Carla Gillis, musician, Toronto
Wendy Gilmour, Gilmour Promotions, Halifax
Andrea Gin, CBC Radio 3, Vancouver
Michel Gionet, Les Disques Imaginaires, Montreal
Émilie Girard, music fan, Quebec City
Michael Godel, music fan, Toronto
Greg Godovitz, musician, Calgary
Gary "Pig" Gold, writer/editor, New York City
Terry Gorman, writer, Moncton
Paul Grady, musician, Toronto
Jeff Graham, KISS-FM, Ottawa
Adam Grant, music journalist, Burlington
Dallas Green, musician, St. Catharines
Melissa Gregerson, S.L. Feldman & Associates, Vancouver
Justin Grenier, music fan, Montreal
Andy Grigg, *Real Blues Magazine*, Victoria
Fish Griwkowsky, critic/photographer, Edmonton
Manny Groneveldt, MuchMusic, Toronto

Robert Gronfors, road manager, Hamilton
R.J. Guha, Kindling Music, Toronto
Cécile Haeffelé, Regroupement artistique francophone de l'Alberta, Edmonton
Doc Halen, CHEZ, Ottawa
Marilyn Hall, music fan, Oakville
Bob Hallett, musician, St. John's
Caitlin Hanford, musician, Toronto
Michael Hanson, musician, Saskatoon
Jane Harbury, Jane Harbury Publicity, Toronto
Chris Harding, BX 93, London
Barbara Harmer, War Child Canada, Toronto
Mavis Harris, FLIP Publicity, Toronto
Roger Harris, Vapor Music, Toronto
Stephanie Harris, Watchdog Management, Vancouver
Tom Harrison, *The Province*, Vancouver
Ron Harwood, EMI Music, Edmonton
Zoe Hawnt, Stony Plain Music, Edmonton
Andrea Hay, music fan, Calgary
Bill Hayes, Q107, Toronto
Reg Hayes, musician, Fredericton
David Hayman, Vapor Music, Toronto
Leitha Haysom, CKBW, Bridgewater, NS
Cara Heath, With A Bullet, Toronto
Sandy Hebenstreit, music blogger, Boca Raton, FL
Louis Hébert, music fan, Montreal
Peter Hemminger, *Fast Forward Weekly*, Calgary
Kathryn Hickling, music fan, Scarborough
Steve Hickling, music fan, Scarborough
Little Miss Higgins, musician, Nokomis, SK
Brad Hilgers, CJSD, Thunder Bay
Julie Hill, The Blues Doctor, Toronto
Mike Hill, Mariposa Folk Festival, Toronto
Jonathan Hille, CHOQ-FM, Montreal
Kevin Hilliard, writer/musician, Toronto
Noyan Hilmi, City Mouse Records, Toronto
Dave Hoddinott, HMV, Fredericton
Mathieu Leblanc Houle, CFOU, Trois-Rivières
Kevin "Sipreano" Howes, producer/manager/deejay, Vancouver
Joanne Huffa, writer/editor, Toronto

Shawn Hughes, Astral Media Radio, Toronto
Colin Hunter, *The Record*, Kitchener-Waterloo
Jeff Hutcheson, CTV's *Canada AM*, Toronto
Sharon Hyland, CHOM-FM, Montreal
Ron Hynes, musician, St. John's
Reid Jamieson, musician, Vancouver
Shuyler Jansen, musician, Saskatoon
Diane Jaroway, Rock 94, Thunder Bay
Greg Jarvis, HMV, St. John's
Michael Jarvis, Universal Music, Toronto
Codi Jeffreys, Majic 100, Ottawa
Nic Jennings, music writer/filmmaker, Toronto
Brian Johnson, The String Guy, Toronto
C. David Johnson, actor/broadcaster/roadie (former), Toronto
Gordie Johnson, musician, Austin, TX
Randy Johnston, Molten Core Records & Collectibles, Toronto
Melanie Jollymore, publicist, Halifax
Catherine Jones, Universal Music, Toronto
Danko Jones, musician, Toronto
Gareth Jones, Upper Class Recordings, Toronto
Sass Jordan, singer, Montreal
Paul Journet, *La Presse*, Montreal
Anne Joyce, Sennheiser Canada, Pointe-Claire, QC
Al Joynes, Q107, Toronto
Kevin Kane, musician, Vancouver
Steve Kane, Warner Music, Toronto
Alain Karon, musician, Montreal
Peter Katz, musician, Toronto
James Keelaghan, musician, Winnipeg
Declan Kelly, music writer, Stratford
Jadea Kelly, musician, Toronto
Kevin Kelly, Magic 106, Guelph
Kevin Kelly, *The Newfoundland Herald*, St. John's
John Kendle, Uptown, Winnipeg
Dylan Kennett, Pop Montreal, Montreal
Barry Kent, consultant, Mount Uniacke, NS
Grant Kerr, music writer, Victoria
Dan Kershaw, SOCAN, Toronto
Ron Kitchener, Open Road Recordings, Toronto

Heather Kitching, publicist/broadcaster, North Vancouver
Colleen Kitts, publicist, Fredericton
Brenna Knought, Juno Awards, Toronto
Carsten Knox, *The Coast*, Halifax
Kevin Komoda, Bongo Beat Records, Montreal
Ron Korb, musician, Toronto
Imants Krumins, music fan, Hamilton
Geoff Kulawick, True North Records, Burlington
Maude Laberge-Boudreau, Dare to Care Records, Montreal
Nicolas Lacroix, CJMF, Quebec City
Lisa LaDouceur, music journalist, Toronto
Mitch Lafon, *BW & BK*, Ottawa
Kevin Laforest, *Voir*, Montreal
Kirk Lahey, Universal Music, Halifax
Ryan Lalonde, The Wolf 101.5, Peterborough
Krista Lamb-Davidson, music fan, Toronto
Vincent Lafrenaye Lamontagne, MEG, Montreal
Frédéric Lamoureux, Preste, Montreal
Benjamin Landry, music fan, Montreal
Scott Landry, CJMO-FM, Moncton
Wilfred Langmaid, *The Daily Gleaner*, Fredericton
Justin Lanoue, CFUV, Victoria
Florence Lapointe, music fan, Montreal
Jean Lapointe, singer/humorist/actor, Price, QC
Jennifer Larkin, Nettwerk, Vancouver
Grit Laskin, Borealis Records, Toronto
Judith Laskin, Canadian Folk Music Awards, Toronto
Zoe Lavoie, music fan, Montreal
James Law, music fan, Mississauga
Grant Lawrence, CBC Radio 3, Vancouver
Dan Laxer, CJAD, Montreal
Larry LeBlanc, *The LeBlanc Newsletter*, Toronto
Xavier Leblanc, music fan, Montreal
Sarah Leclerc, music fan, Montreal
Alain Lefebvre, CFOU, Trois-Rivières
Marianne Lefebvre, music fan, Montreal
Marie Lefebvre, RockDétante 102.7, Sherbrooke

François Lemay, Espace Musique, Montreal
Bruce Leperre, CKDM, Dauphin, MB
Valérie Lesage, *Le Soleil*, Quebec City
Vincent Lessard, music fan, Montreal
Alana Levandoski, musician, Kelwood, MB
Camille Lévesque, music fan, Montreal
Martin Levin, *The Globe and Mail*, Toronto
David Levinson, Macklam/Feldman Management, Vancouver
Mary Levitan, Macklam/Feldman Management, Vancouver
Eric Lewis, *The Times & Transcript*, Moncton
Jason Lewis, Pyramid Productions, Calgary
Pat Leyland, entertainment lawyer, Toronto
W.D. Lighthall, music fan, Toronto
Colin Linden, musician, Toronto
Cam Lindsay, *Exclaim* magazine, Toronto
Suzanne Little, artist manager, Salt Spring Island, BC
Josef Loderer, music fan, London, UK
Mark Logan, Busted Flat Records, North Kitchener
Craig Lomas, music fan, Burlington
Marie-Josée Longval, RockDétente 107.5, Quebec City
Cara Luft, musician, Calgary
Rob Lutes, musician, Montreal
Nanda Lwin, music writer, London
Ellen Mably, lyricist, Calgary
Ian MacArthur, CHFI, Toronto
Mark MacDonald, music fan, Guelph
Craig MacInnis, music writer, Toronto
Larry MacInnis, CHUM-FM, Toronto
Art MacIntyre, Transistor 66 Record Co., Winnipeg
Jason MacIsaac, musician, Halifax
Rob MacIsaac, musician, Saint-Lazare, QC
Colin MacKenzie, CBC Radio 2, Winnipeg
Carol Maclean, music fan, Vancouver
James Maclean, Talk's Cheap Management, Toronto
Peter MacMartin, music fan, Toronto
Jenna MacNeil, CBC Radio, Toronto
Mike Magee, Union Label Group, Montreal
Ian Mahoney, music fan, Toronto
Cam Malcolm, musician, Hamilton
François Marchand, music writer, Edmonton

Don Marcotte, CKUA, Edmonton
Margaret Marissen, manager, Toronto
Nancy Marley, Justin Time Records, Montreal
Lee Marshall, broadcaster, Temiskaming Shores, ON
Antonio Marsillo, In2 Music, Montreal
Stéphane Martel, *Voir*, Montreal
Zachary Martel, music fan, Montreal
Craig Martin, founder, Classic Albums Live, Toronto
Melissa Martin, music journalist, Winnipeg
Olivier Martin, music fan, Montreal
Bob Martineau, artist manager, Nanaimo
Henry Martinuk, filmmaker, Toronto
Brent Mason, musician, Saint John
Waye Mason, Halifax Pop Explosion, Halifax
Drew Masters, *M.E.A.T Magazine*, Toronto
Keith Maurik, Epitaph Records, Toronto
John Mazerolle, *Here*, Fredericton
Sue McCallum, The Next Level PR & Events, Whitby, ON
Linda McCann, S.L. Feldman & Associates, Vancouver
Scott McCord, CFBR The Bear, Edmonton
Heath McCoy, *The Calgary Herald*, Calgary
Mike McFarland, 89.9 HAL-FM Halifax
Glenn McFarlane, Brampton Folk Club, Brampton
Cody McGraw, *SoundProof Magazine*, Toronto
Arthur McGregor, Ottawa Folklore Centre, Ottawa
Phlis McGregor, CBC Radio, Halifax
David McGugan, music fan, Edmonton
Ra McGuire, musician, Vancouver
Will McGuirk, music writer, Durham Region, ON
Trent McMartin, music writer, Edmonton
John McMaster, Capitol Theatre, Moncton
Bob McNeil, music collector, Halifax
Nat Merenda, K.Pone Inc. Music Group, Montreal
Andy Ramesh Meyers, musician, Toronto
Philippe Michaud, music fan, Montreal
Greg Mikolas, Canadian Classic Rock, Regina

Carolyn Mill, manager, Victoria
Lisa Millar, music consultant, Ottawa
Brandi Mills, Canadian Country Music Association, Toronto
Mark Milne, Sonic Unyon Records, Hamilton
Jess Milton, CBC Radio's *The Vinyl Cafe*, Toronto
Francis Mineau, musician, Montreal
Jason Mingo, musician, Halifax
Mister Zero, musician, Oakville
Don Mitchell, CFNY, Toronto
Jennifer Moisan, Zone3 Disques & Spectacles, Montreal
Lou Molinaro, promoter, Hamilton
James Monaco, publicist, Haileybury, ON
Michael Moniz, musician, Hamilton
Sam Moon, musician, Dartmouth
Éric Moreault, *Le Soleil*, Quebec City
Heather Morgan, musician/filmmaker, Toronto
Jeffery Morgan, *CREEM*, Detroit
Chloe Morin, music fan, Montreal
Andrea Morris, AM to FM Promotions, Toronto
Tracey Morris, music fan, Toronto
Gerry Mosby, Vapor Music, Toronto
Jeremy Mosher, music fan, Calgary
Richard Moule, journalist, London
Bruce Mowat, Audio-Video Sales, Grand Prairie, AB
Christine Mulkins, Boost PR, Toronto
Jenny Mulkins, music fan, Toronto
Eden Munro, *Vue Weekly*, Edmonton
Bill Munson, Music Fan, Toronto
Samuel Murdock, musician, Quebec City
Tom Mureika, publicist, Ucluelet, BC
Brendan Murphy, music columnist, Montreal
Java Joel Murphy, 94.7 Hits FM, Montreal
Marty Murray, musician, Niagara Falls
Tyler Myalls, recording engineer, Halifax
David Myles, musician, Halifax
Alex Nadeau, music fan, Montreal
Troy Neilson, musician, Ottawa
Eileen Neumann, CHUM-FM, Toronto
Evan Newman, manager, Toronto

Steve Nightingale, Universal Music, Toronto
Annie Nikolajevich, music fan, Toronto
Allen Nolan, music fan, Ottawa
Barry Norris, Barry's Discs, Lower Kingsclear, NB
Ian North, musician, Kitchener
Peter North, CKUA, Edmonton
Craig Northey, musician, Vancouver
Ronan O'Leary, Beggars Group, Toronto
Mike O'Neill, musician, Halifax
Seamus O'Regan, CTV's *Canada AM*, Toronto
Terry O'Reilly, Pirate Radio, Toronto
Heather Ostertag, Factor, Toronto
Étienne Ouellet, music fan, Sherbrooke
Phillippe Ouellette, music fan, Montreal
Mark Owen, Indie Guitar Co., Cornwall
Les Palango, C101, Hamilton
Sean Palmerston, Sonic Unyon Records, Hamilton
Dave Panting, musician, St. John's
Sofi Papamarko, music writer, Toronto
Jacob Paquette, music fan, Montreal
Yves Paquette, Astral Media, Sherbrooke
Sebastien Paquin, Bonsound, Montreal
Kelly Parker, 99.9 BOB-FM, Winnipeg
Zak Pashak, Sled Island Festival, Calgary
Nate Patrin, music writer, St. Paul, MN
Vincent Peake, musician, Montreal
Simon Pelletier, music fan, Montreal
André Péloquin, BangBangBlog, Montreal
Roland Pemberton, musician, Edmonton
Marc Perry, EMI Music, Halifax
Michael Persaud, music fan, Toronto
Bernard Perusse, *The Gazette*, Montreal
Holger Petersen, Stony Plain Records, Edmonton
Mike Petkau, Head In The Sand Productions, Winnipeg
Heidi Petracek, CBC-TV, Halifax
Shawn Petsche, Shed Island Festival, Calgary
Wayne Petti, musician, Toronto
Wendy Phillips, Sonic Entertainment, Halifax
Carole Pigeon, Canadian Folk Music Awards, Verchères, QC

Uncle Rob Pinnock, The Fox, Fredericton
Sandra Plagakis, KISS-FM, Ottawa
Léa Noémie Plourde-Arche, CHOQ-FM, Montreal
Ghislain Poirier, musician, Montreal
Guillaume Poirier, music fan, Hull, QC
John Poirier, Warner Music, Halifax
Silas Polkinghorne, journalist, Victoria
Bryan Potvin, producer/musician, Toronto
Eve Poulin, music fan, Montreal
Colleen Power, musician, St. John's
Tim Powis, Bravo!, Toronto
Steve Pratt, CBC Radio 3, Ottawa
Steve Profenna, musician, Toronto
Doug Proulx, musician/broadcaster, Vancouver
Amanda Putz, CBC Radio 3, Ottawa
Al Quint, Suburan Voice Blog, Peabody, MA
Michel Quintal, Piknic Electronik, Montreal
Elana Rabinovitch, Propaganda Ink, Toronto
Dave Rave, musician, Hamilton
James Reaney, *The London Free Press*, London
Chris Reichardt, music fan, Calgary
Bob Reid, CFRB, Toronto
Pat Reid, Warner Music, Toronto
Scott Remila, musician, City and Colour/ The Violet Archers, Toronto
Nathalie Renault, musician, Campbellton, NB
Dan Reynish, CBC Radio, Regina
Mark Rheaume, CBC Radio, Toronto
Adam Ricard, 102.1 The Edge, Toronto
Nicolas Richard, music fan, Montreal
Jay Richards, CJWW, Saskatoon
Mike Richards, CKBW, Bridgewater, NS
Daniel Richler, broadcaster/author, London, UK
Jeff Rioux, *Emoragei*, Montreal
Maxim Roberge, RockDétente, Chicoutimi
Mark Roberts, Capitol FM, Fredericton
Sam Roberts, musician, Montreal
Dale Robertson, Universal Music, Vancouver
Daniel Robichaud, Sony Music, Halifax

Samantha Robichaud, musician, Riverview, NB
Andrew Robinson, Last Gang Records, Toronto
Paul Robinson, musician, London, UK
Tom Robinson, music fan, Calgary
Simon Robitaille, Taxi Promo, Montreal
Brian Roche, musician, Vancouver
Graham Rockingham, *The Hamilton Spectator*, Hamilton
Robert Ross, CFOM, Quebec City
Sean Ross, Edison Media Research, Somerville, NJ
Emma Roy, music fan, Montreal
Léo Roy, music fan, Sherbrooke
Sean Russell, manager, Toronto
Justin Rutledge, musician, Toronto
Catherine St. Germain, musician, Winnipeg
Gabriel St.-Pierre, music fan, Montreal
Wendy Salsman, goddess, Halifax
Steven Sandor, *Vue Weekly*, Toronto
Paul Sarazin, music fan, Aurora, ON
Bob Sato, music fan, Toronto
Drew Savage, Virgin Radio, Richmond
Guillaume Savard, Énergie 98.7, Rimouski
Tonia Schroepfer, music fan, Calgary
Franz Schuller, musician, Montreal
Ingrid Schumacher, CHUM-FM, Toronto
Justin Sconci, music fan, Mississauga
Ian Scott, music writer, Calgary
Meghan Scott, Tuck and Roll Productions, Fredericton
Erica Seaman, music fan, Vancouver
Bryce Seefieldt, Offshoot Communications, Toronto
Daniel Seligman, Pop Montreal, Montreal
Jay Semko, musician, Saskatoon
Sonia Sennik, music journalist, Hamilton
Anne Sérode, Espace musique, Montreal
Tony Servello, Fontana North, Toronto
Ron Sexsmith, musician, Toronto
Sander Shalinsky, lawyer/manager, Toronto
Paul Shaver, EMI Music, Toronto
Kevin Shea, former music industry executive, Toronto
Adam Shetler, music fan, Calgary
Elodie Simard, music fan, Trois-Rivières
Steve Simmons, *The Toronto Sun*, Toronto

Paola Simonetto, Musique Plus, Montreal
Peter Sisk, musician, Hamilton
Lorie Slater, Universal Music, Toronto
Sarah Slean, musician, Toronto
Tara Slone, musician, The Joys, Toronto
Doug Smith, musician, Vancouver
Graham Smith, music fan, Winnipeg
Nat Smith, music fan, Winnipeg
Sarah Smith, musician, The Joys, London
Elizabeth Spear, Ole, Toronto
Dave Spencer, Eggplant Management, Toronto
Sandra Sperounes, *The Edmonton Journal*, Edmonton
Brent Staeben, Harvest Jazz And Blues Festival, Fredericton
Graham Stairs, Finkelstein Management, Toronto
Connie Stefanson, marketing/event consultant, Hamilton
Mark Steinmetz, CBC Radio, Toronto
Darryl Sterdan, *The Winnipeg Sun*, Winnipeg
Darryl Stevens, Giant 101.9, Sydney
Bill Stevenson, retailer, Kingston
Rick Stevenson, music fan, Calgary
Pat Steward, musician, Vancouver
Warren Stewart, EMI Music, Toronto
Jayme Stone, musician, Toronto
Stu Strang, music fan, Halifax
Michael Stroh, festival music manager, Toronto
Mark Swierszcz, MuchMusic, Toronto
Daniel Sylvester, BOB FM, Ottawa
Jowi Taylor, Six String Nation, Toronto
Ric Taylor, music writer/broadcaster, Hamilton
Charles Teed, musician, Saint John
Paul Templeman, CBC-TV, Toronto
William "Skinny" Tenn, Hardwood Records, Toronto
James Tennant, McMaster Radio, Hamilton
John Terry, musician, Glace Bay, NS
Éric Theriault, music writer, Montreal
Alexis Thibault, music fan, Montreal
Marc Thivierge, manager, Montreal
Doug Thompson, Douglas Communications, Toronto
Laura Thompson, CBC-TV, Toronto

Holly Thorne, Q92, Sudbury
John Threlfall, music writer, Victoria
Joanne Tickle, filmmaker/musician, Hastings, ON
Martin Tielli, musician, Toronto
Jordan Timm, music writer, Toronto
Elly Tose, Elster Productions, Thunder Bay
Mike Trebilcock, musician, Hamilton
Alexandre Tremblay, music fan, Montreal
Georges Tremblay, Dep Distribution, Montreal
Noémie Tremblay, music fan, Montreal
Brad Trew, Cyclone Records, Aurora, ON
Chris Trowbridge, CBC-TV, Toronto
Éric Trudel, author/journalist, Montreal
Jenny Usher, KISS-FM, Ottawa
Pierre Vachon, Radio Énergie, Gatineau, PQ
François Valenti, Radio Énergie, Quebec City
Mathieu Valiquette, Archambault, Montreal
Jim Vallance, musician, Vancouver
Vickie Van Dyke, The Wave, Hamilton
Tanya VanLuven, Warner Music, Toronto
Jaime Vernon, *The Canadian Pop Encyclopedia*, Toronto
Roy Henry Vickers, Eagle Dancer Enterprises, Hazelton, BC

LoriAnn Villani, The Edge, Toronto
Manon Vincent, musician, Montreal
Guy Violette, music fan, Fredericton
Eric Volmers, *The Calgary Herald*, Calgary
Kim Wagner, The Voice, Kitchener
Alex J. Walling, Queens County Community Radio, Liverpool, NS
Jesse Wanagas, music fan, Toronto
Park Warden, The Bear, Edmonton
Betty Watson, music fan, Ottawa
Mark Watson, manager, Toronto
Jeff Weaver, announcer (retired), London
Shannon Webb-Campbell, journalist, Halifax
Allan Webster, Select Distribution, Toronto
Wayne Webster, Virgin Radio, Toronto
Grant Weir, Cineplex Entertainment, Toronto
Matt Wells, MuchMusic, Toronto
Adam West, Hot 103, Winnipeg
John Westhaver, Birdman Sound, Ottawa
Gail Wetton, Molten Core Records & Collectibles, Toronto
Chris White, CJAM 91.5 FM, Windsor
Tim White, music fan, Montreal
Allan Wigney, *The Ottawa Sun*, Ottawa
John Wiles, CKBW, Bridgewater, NS
Andy Wilson, CBC-TV, Fredericton

Anya Wilson, Anya Wilson Publicity, Toronto
Carl Wilson, *The Globe and Mail*, Toronto
Tom Wilson, musician, Hamilton
Jen Winsor, Music Industry Association of Newfoundland and Labrador, St. John's
Adele Wolfe, musician, Tilley, AB
Eric Woodruff, Universal Music, Toronto
Jeff Woods, host, *The Legends of Classic Rock*, Toronto
Scott Woods, rockcritics.com, Toronto
Ed Woodsworth, producer/musician, Albert Bridge, NS
Michael Wrycraft, artwork designer, Toronto
Les Yatabe, music fan, Toronto
Ted Yates, Radio Astral, Hamilton
Tim Yerxa, executive director, The Playhouse, Fredericton
Miles Yohnke, Patrick 5 Star Productions, Saskatoon
Ritchie Yorke, music writer, Australia
Stewart Young, CBC Radio, Halifax
Anna Zee, Q104, Halifax
Matt Zimbel, musician, Montreal
Gillian Zulauf, North X Northeast, Toronto

Acknowledgements

My great thanks once again to the staff of Goose Lane Editions, who have worked so hard over the course of two books, this one and *The Top 100 Canadian Albums*. They have been firm supporters of the idea of presenting Canadian music as an equal art form, deserving of the highest-quality publication. The presentation of this book is a tribute to their dedication.

Special thanks go to designer Kent Fackenthall, who made this book a visual treat for music fans. So many people have told me *The Top 100 Canadian Albums* has stayed on their coffee tables since it first came out, and that I believe is a tribute to Kent's work.

Editor Barry Norris returned to the team for this book, and once again made what is supposed to be the most excruciating part of the process, in fact, one of the most pleasant. His interest, encouragement, and praise kept me pumped up at every turn. He also kept me focused on the facts, which is what music fans want.

Sue McCallum of The Next Level PR & Events is more than a publicist; she is a great friend. Her enthusiasm for the project and all my music work lifts me at just the right times. The success of her work in placing me on television, radio, websites, and print from coast to coast speaks for itself.

At times I ran into brick walls, and then some very good friends came to my aid. Cheers especially to Jaimie Vernon, the creator of *The Canadian Pop Music Encyclopedia*, who knew phone numbers, had the 45s, and always had the right help almost instantly. John Einarson is one of the best music writers working today (just ask *Mojo* and *Uncut* magazines), and was more than generous with his contacts. Ralph Alphonso is an institution — a poet, publisher, label owner, and, above all, a fan — and was happy to make the connections for me. Larry Leblanc simply knows all and everyone, and I thank him for his support and sharing. Jennifer Sweet provided some important research and explanation, and I even borrowed a couple of lines on a tough subject. Sharon Hudson did some quick but tough translation when she was supposed to be working. Colleen Kitts stopped me from making a fool of myself, and offered up some better writing than my own. Maggie Estey strongarmed some Montreal voters. Heather Kitching kept me afloat.

The music industry in Canada is a large and vibrant family, and I've been lucky enough to make hundreds of friends across the country. They are the key to such a large project, and it's a joy to be able to call on so many wonderful people, from music company employees to the media to the musicians themselves. The list of jurors includes friends old and new, and many of the people to whom I am closest in life. I thank each and every one.

I also called on lots of people to help set up interviews and to acquire photos and clearances. So, once again, a big thanks to: Kari Atwell, Julie Baldwin, Cynthia Barry, Ken Beattie, Karen Bliss, Kathryn Blythe, Janesta Boudreau, Carole Boutin, Keith Brown, Gérard Brunet, Dave Buerster, Marie-Christine Champagne, Jon Conrad, Jude Coombe, Andy Curran, Louise Curtis, Frank Davies, Gourmet Délice, Vince Ditrich, George Elmes, Bernie Finkelstein, Richard Flohil, Roy Forbes, Diane Foy, Wayne Francis, Ivan Hicks, Lynn Horne, Sheri Jones, Daniel Keebler, Geoff Kulawick, Ronald Labelle, Maude Laberge-Boudreau, Gail Lagden, Kirk Lahey, Johanne Leblanc, Anna LeCoche, Anne Liebold, Angus MacKay, Margaret Marissen, Christian Michaels, Dounia Mikou, Jess Milton, Jessica Moore, Christy Newman, Magali Ould, Mark Perry, Holger Petersen, Christine Pietz, John Poirier, Jenn Pressey, Dianne Reid, Daniel Robichaud, Étienne Roy, Jonathan Simkin, Graham Stairs, Charles Stewart, Michelle Szeto, David Tysowski, Jim Vallance, Nicoleta Varlan, Euvin Weeber, and Jessica Zambri.

Finally, this book is for my sons, who impress everyone they meet and have grown to become wonderful friends to each other and to me. Their mother has instilled a tremendous sense of good in each of them, and I know they will grow to be excellent young men. The boys and Colleen gave me countless hours to work on these books, which I owe them in the future. So, this work is dedicated to Evan, Aidan, and Ben.

Every effort has been made to secure permission for photographs and illustrations reproduced in this book from the rightful copyright holders. We regret any inadvertent omission.

Top 100: Artist Photos
Introduction: With permission of Ranbach Music Ltd.; Courtesy: Janesta Boudreau; Courtesy: Kirk Lahey; Courtesy: Alan Katowitz / 1. With permission of Ranbach Music Ltd.; With permission of Ranbach Music Ltd. / 2. Photo by Steve Babineau, Courtesy of Warner Music Canada; Courtesy of Warner Music Canada / 3. Photo by Elliott Landy; Photo by Elliott Landy / 4. Photo by Otto Scheut / 5. Photo by John Rowlands; Image Provided Courtesy of Sony Music Entertainment Canada Inc.; Image Provided Courtesy of Sony Music Entertainment Canada Inc. / 6. Photo by John Rowlands, Courtesy of MCA Records Inc. / 7. Photo by John Reeves, Courtesy of Warner Music Canada; Photo by John Rowlands; Courtesy of Warner Music Canada / 8. With permission of Ranbach Music Ltd.; With permission of Ranbach Music Ltd. / 9. Courtesy of Vanguard Records Archive; Photo by John Rowlands / 10. Courtesy: Rich Dodson; Photo by John Rowlands / 11. Photo by John Rowlands / 12. Photo by Fin Costello, Courtesy of Anthem / 13. Courtesy of Starfish Entertainment / 14. Photo by Richard Beland / 15. Photo by John Rowlands / 16. Photo by Bob Cato, Image Provided Courtesy of Sony Music Entertainment Canada Inc. / 17. Courtesy of EMI Music Canada / 18. With permission of Ranbach Music Ltd. / 19. Photo by Joseph Sia, Courtesy of Warner Music Canada / 20. Photo by Catherine Stockhausen / 21. Photo by Elliott Landy / 22. Photo by Steve Carty, Courtesy Wesley Williams aka Maestro Fresh Wes; Photo by Steve Carty, Courtesy Wesley Williams aka Maestro Fresh Wes / 23. Courtesy: Ralph Alfonso / 24. Courtesy of Universal Music Canada; Photo by Fin Costello, Courtesy of Anthem / 25. Photo by Bruce Cole, Courtesy the Frank Davies Archives / 26. Courtesy of Finkelstein Management Company Ltd. / 27. Courtesy of Muffin Music / 28. Courtesy of Rich Dodson / 29. Credit: Gabriel Jones / 30. Courtesy of Warner Music Canada; Courtesy

of Warner Music Canada / 31. Ronald Labelle Photography / 32. Courtesy: Moe Berg / 33. Photo by Ivan Creighton / 34. Photo by Catherine Stockhausen / 35. Photo by Fin Costello, Courtesy of Anthem / 36. Courtesy: Gord Lewis / 37. With permission of Ranbach Music Ltd. / 38. Courtesy: Gary Latendresse and Five Man Electrical Band (www.fivemanelectricalband.ca) / 39. Photo by John Bentham / 40. Courtesy: Connie Hynes; Photo by Martin Laba / 41. Courtesy: Ivan Doroschuk (photograph) / 42. grahamkennedy.ca; grahamkennedy.ca / 43. Photo by John Rowlands / 44. Photo by Joel Brodsky, Courtesy The Frank Davies Archives / 45. Courtesy of Aquarius Records / 47. Courtesy: Ra McGuire / 48. Photo by Dimo Safari, Image Provided Courtesy of Sony Music Entertainment Canada Inc. / 49. Photo by Deborah Samuel, Courtesy of Warner Music Canada / 50. Photo by John Rowlands / 51. Photo by Joseph Yarmush / 53. Courtesy of Warner Music Canada / 54. © 2007 Mary Rozzi / 55. Credit: Gabriel Jones / 56. Photo by Herb Ritts, Courtesy of Warner Music Canada / 57. Photo by Jay Blakesberg, Courtesy of Warner Music Canada / 58. Photo by John Rowlands / 59. Courtesy of Finkelstein Management Company Ltd. / 60. Courtesy of Universal Music Canada / 61. Courtesy: Alan Katowitz / 62. Original Artwork by Lyndon Andrews, Courtesy of Ready Records / 63. Courtesy of A&M Records Inc. / 64. Courtesy of Universal Music Canada / 65. Photo by Jay Strauss / 66. from "Hank's Favourite Songs No 4" Canadian Music Sales Corp Ltd. circa 1940s / 68. Courtesy of MCA Records Inc. / 70. Image Provided Courtesy of Sony Music Entertainment Canada Inc. / 71. © 2007 Moo, Courtesy of EMI Music Canada / 72. Courtesy of The Kings / 73. Courtesy of Warner Music Canada / 74. José Enrique Montes Hernandez / 75. Photographer unknown. Used by permission of Paul Hyde. / 76. Courtesy of Starfish Entertainment / 77. With permission of Ranbach Music Ltd. / 78. Courtesy of Finkelstein Management Company Ltd. / 79. Photo by John Rowlands / 81. Photo by Alan Katowitz / 82. Courtesy of Ra McGuire / 83. Photo by John Rowlands / 84. Ronald Labelle Photography / 86. Courtesy of Stompin' Tom Connors and Canada Post Corporation © Canada Post Corporation, 2009 / 87. Photo by Richard Beland, Courtesy of Universal Music Canada / 88. Ronald Labelle Photography / 89. Courtesy of Warner Music Canada / 90. Photo by Erica Henderson / 91. With permission of Ranbach Music Ltd. / 92. Photo by Gerard "Junior" Brunet / 93. Photo by John Rowlands / 94. Image Provided Courtesy of Sony Music Entertainment Canada Inc. / 95. Photo by Adam Vollick / 98. Courtesy of Warner Music Canada / 100. Courtesy of The Tom Kotter Company/One Four Seven Records

Top 100: Cover Art & 45 Labels
1. Image Provided Courtesy of Sony Music Entertainment Canada Inc.; Image Provided Courtesy of Sony Music Entertainment Canada Inc. / 3. Courtesy of EMI Music Canada / 4. Courtesy of A&M Records Inc.; Courtesy of A&M Records Inc. / 5. Image Provided Courtesy of Sony Music Entertainment Canada Inc. / 6. Courtesy of MCA Records Inc. / 10. Courtesy of EMI Music Canada / 13. Courtesy of Warner Music Canada / 15. Courtesy of Warner Music Canada / 18. Image Provided Courtesy of Sony Music Entertainment Canada Inc. / 19. Courtesy of Warner Music Canada / 20. Photo by Laura Borealis / 21. Courtesy of EMI Music Canada; Courtesy of EMI Music Canada / 25. Courtesy The Frank Davies Archives / 27. Courtesy of EMI Music Canada / 33. Courtesy Dave Bingham / 34. Photo by Michael Halsband / 36. Courtesy: Gord Lewis / 38. Courtesy of Polydor Records / 41. Courtesy of Warner Music Canada / 45. Courtesy of Aquarius Records / 46. Image Provided Courtesy of Sony Music Entertainment Canada Inc.; Image Provided Courtesy of Sony Music Entertainment Canada Inc. / 48. Image Provided Courtesy of Sony Music Entertainment Canada Inc. / 50. Courtesy of Terry Jacks (Gone Fishin' Music Ltd.) / 52. Courtesy of Warner Music Canada / 63. Courtesy of A&M Records Inc. / 67. Courtesy of Universal Music Canada / 69. Photo by Catherine Stockhausen / 80. Courtesy of Gord Lewis / 85. Courtesy of A&M Records Inc. / 96. Original Graphics by Dean Motter, Photos by P.L. Noble, Courtesy of Ready Records 97. Courtesy of EMI Music Canada / 99. Courtesy of A&M Records Inc.

Index